Tea goes everywhere . . .

Even to the top of the world, where Tibetans civilize life in the frozen Himalayas with a hot cup of tea. Strong and steeped for an hour, Tibetan tea does not resemble the clear amber or green drink sipped by English queens and Japanese emperors. Quantities of salt are added to the tea. It is then churned with butter made from the milk of a yak, the mountains' long-haired beast of burden. The smell is not delicate, the color is muddied with butter fat. But it is tea, body-warming, soul-embracing tea . . .

Hot or iced, black or green, scented, spiced or flavored—*Loving Tea* is a comprehensive guide to the basic and finer points of tea. With brewing tips, recipes, and more, it takes you on a tour of the wide world of tea—and shows you how to bring it home to your very own kitchen.

D0789468

Loving Tea

JANE RESNICK

BERKLEY BOOKS, NEW YORK

Excerpt by Dylan Thomas, from UNDER MILK WOOD. Copyright © 1954 by New Directions Publishing Corp. Reprinted by permission of New Directions Publishing Corp.

LOVING TEA

A Berkley Book / published by arrangement with
the author

PRINTING HISTORY
Berkley edition / December 1997

All rights reserved.
Copyright © 1997 by Jane Resnick.
Book design by Casey Hampton.
This book may not be reproduced in whole
or in part, by mimeograph or any other means,
without permission. For information address:
The Berkley Publishing Group, a member of Penguin Putnam Inc.,
200 Madison Avenue, New York, New York 10016.

The Putnam Berkley World Wide Web site address is
http://www.berkley.com

ISBN: 0-425-16119-6

BERKLEY®
Berkley Books are published by the Berkley Publishing Group,
a member of Penguin Putnam Inc.,
200 Madison Avenue, New York, New York 10016.
BERKLEY and the "B" design are trademarks belonging to
Berkley Publishing Corporation.

PRINTED IN THE UNITED STATES OF AMERICA

10 9 8 7 6 5 4 3 2 1

It has been well said that tea is suggestive of a thousand wants, from which spring the decencies and luxuries of civilization.

—AGNES REPPLIER (1858–1950)

Contents

THE PERFECT CUP: MAKING TEA

THE ART AND SCIENCE OF TEA

HERBAL TEAS

TEA CEREMONIES: ANCIENT AND ONE'S OWN

CONTENTS

THE TEA PARTY: RECIPES FOR ACCOMPANIMENTS

The Journey of Tea

Taming Wild Tea: How Tea Grows

Tea, unlike money, *does* grow on trees, but the journey from leaf to cup is an arduous one. In growing tea, man cultivates his finest instincts, harnessing nature to enhance the quality of his life in the most civilized manner. It's been centuries since we ascended from the caveman's campfire to the gentleman's parlor—and tea is one of the things that got us there.

TWO THOUSAND TEAS

The tea plant, *Camellia sinensis,* is a flowering evergreen shrub with over 2,000 varieties—and therein lie the possibilities for untold nuances in your cup. Tea is compared to wine in this regard, for just as no two grapes, grown in different places, are exactly alike, no two types of tea, raised in varied terrain, will brew with the same color, fragrance, and flavor. Exploring this extravagance of riches is the pleasure of the tea drinker.

On its own, *Camellia sinensis* grows wild and is not finicky about where. It is indigenous to the land that is now China,

Tibet, and northern India. A hardy plant, the tea bush sprouts in sandy or clay soils but not swamps. Heat and humidity are its optimum growing conditions. Therefore, commercial tea occurs in tropical and subtropical territories where the weather is warm (up to 95° F) and the rainfall is plentiful (up to 100 inches a year). That puts tea, for the most part, in jungles not far from the equator. However, there is a paradox. Although tea grows most abundantly in these areas, the finest teas flourish in the rarefied, cooler atmosphere of altitude— 3,000 to 7,000 feet and up. Tea grown in India, Sri Lanka, and Kenya as high as 6,000 feet is some of the best in the world. On these mountaintops, tea does a balancing act; the lower temperatures induce slow growth and produce a richer, more complex leaf, but a precipitous drop in degrees can be disastrous.

THE CULTIVATED CROP

On slopes or plains, tea territory has a genteel nomenclature all its own. Tea never grows on ranches or farms, but always on *plantations, estates,* or *gardens,* no matter how large or small the acreage. The contour of the land dictates the planting, and sensibly so. In steep areas, tea bushes are terraced, carving out swirls on the mountainside. On flat land, rows and rows carpet the landscape with as many as 3,000 to 4,000 an acre planted four feet apart. Shade trees stand like sentinels among the valuable bushes, shielding them from scorching sun, monsoons, winds, or whatever calamities nature is wont to impose.

PRUNED TO PERFECTION

As with all agricultural enterprises, hard work is the oil of the tea engine, and much of it is still done by hand. Seeds, of course, are the first step, and these are hovered over in a nursery until the plants are six to eighteen months old when they are set out in the tea gardens. Tea can also be planted by *cloning,* which is not as futuristic as it sounds, but merely the planting of a mature leaf in the ground, no gene manipulation required. As the bush develops, man steps into the natural process early with a sharply curved knife that makes all the difference. Pruning is the key to tea growing. Left on its own, *Camellia sinensis* becomes a tree, a sixty-foot tree, with nothing to show for its growth but height. Its leaves would be useless for tea. So each young tree is continually cut back into a bush, three or four feet high and wide. Several years of pruning are necessary—about three years for bushes at lower elevations and as many as five for those in the hills—before the plants are ready for leaf harvesting. This constant clipping forces the plant to produce young leaves. It is only these young leaves that are reborn in a cup to become tea.

THE TENDER FLUSH

They are called the *flush*. The flush is two tender, young leaves and a small, unopened leaf bud—therein lies all the potential for what the tea will become. The traditional method of harvesting the flush is *plucking,* and it's done by the deft hands of women who wend their way through the waist-high bushes, snipping the tips of tea branches with their thumb and forefinger. Carrying baskets on their backs or heads, each plucker can pick about 30,000 shoots a day, perhaps as much as forty pounds of leaf, which will be transformed into about ten pounds of processed tea leaves.

In hot, humid climates, a flush may occur every seven or eight days; in cooler areas, the number of flushes can be seasonal. Some contemporary tea growers have attempted to replace this skilled handpicking by machines, but like many changes made in the name of efficiency, the outcomes have been questionable. Tea resists modernization, or perhaps it transcends changes wrought by man and endures as a reminder that true essences are timeless and immutable. Thus, plucked by hand, the leaves are ready for a process that has remained essentially the same for centuries.

Torturing for Taste: How Tea Is Manufactured

Thank god for Tea! What would the world do without tea! How did it exist? I am glad I was not born before tea.

—SIDNEY SMITH (1711–1845)

Nothing seems simpler than a steaming, clear liquid in a cup. Yet, what we ask from tea is hardly simple. In a sip, we expect it to lift our spirits, rejuvenate our energies, warm our bodies, soothe our aches, enhance our thoughts, stimulate our palates, and cultivate our conversations—sometimes all at once. Tea is up to these demands, but not on its own. A leaf going straight from tree to cup is not at all the drink we know. Actually, it's undrinkable. As natural as tea is, the leaves we infuse are the product of human intervention, ancient practices that have never been fully mechanized and still require man's judgments and sensibilities. There are "tea men" behind every cup you brew.

THE RIGHT PLUCK

Even the first step, plucking the leaves from the bush, involves weighing factors and making choices. With each flush, growers must make decisions about how early to pick and what leaves to take. The first two new leaves and the bud are most commonly plucked, but a grower may decide on a smaller harvest and pluck just the bud and next youngest leaf. These will produce a finer, rarer tea. On the other hand, he could choose to pluck the bud, two new leaves, and the older leaf just below, and gain in quantity what he loses in quality. The factors mount. Not all flushes are created equal; the earliest of each season is the finest. Plucking must be uniform; a mixing of sizes will do a tea in. From the moment a leaf is plucked, its final character is being determined.

Mention must be made of the fact that hands are not doing all of the plucking these days. Machines have come to the tea garden. Few places on the planet have resisted mechanization for so long, but some estates have succumbed. They have replaced the orthodox method of hand plucking with what has come to be known as the CTC or cut-torn-crushed process. However, we should indulge in neither judgment nor despair and acknowledge that the broken leaves obtained when CTC is applied properly can produce some very fine, rapid-infusing cups of tea.

FERMENTATION: THE KEY TO TEA

Any leaf can be become one of the three basic types of tea: *black* tea (which is called red in China), *green* tea, or *oolong*. The key to the differences is fermentation. Black is fermented, green is unfermented, and oolong is semifermented.

During fermentation, the natural process of oxidation occurs, altering the chemistry of the leaf and developing the essential oils that determine the body, strength, flavor, and color of a tea. That's nature's part. The manufacturing strives to capture the tea at its peak moment in this process and then dry it, thus preserving the tea at its best until it meets boiling water in your cup. The steps in the manufacturing procedure are centuries old, proof that new technology doesn't have the answer for *everything*. They are: withering, rolling, roll-breaking, fermentation, and firing.

STEP BY STEP TO TEA

Black tea, which is created in the process described below, undergoes the greatest transformation from its natural state.

Withering occurs right after plucking. The tea leaves are spread out on racks to dry for eighteen to twenty-four hours. It seems to be an axiom that tea should not be hurried in either its drinking or its manufacturing. During this time, which the tea dictates—man has never been able to hurry this along—the leaves lose a great deal of their moisture and that's the point. They wither and soften. The leaves need to be pliable or they'll tear during the next step, which is rolling.

Rolling is done by a rather low-tech machine that crushes and twists the leaves, breaking up the plant cells and releasing the juices and enzymes that are responsible for a tea's characteristic flavor. A lot happens here that your taste buds will eventually appreciate. During this tumbling and bruising, oxidation begins and the essential oils start developing. And the leaves get their *twist*—some will curl up and others lay flat. This shape is not a matter of aesthetics, but taste, because, at this stage, the balance between flavor and pungency in the final tea begins to take shape. How a leaf is twisted counts in the rate in which it will infuse, which helps to balance the final mix.

Roll-breaking is next because, battered as they are in the rolling, the leaves form clumps. Machines called ball-breakers go to work on the twisted-up clumps, separating the leaves and sifting them for size. Uniform size is important so each group of tea will ferment evenly. At this point, the tea is, as one might imagine, as languid as a noodle, soft and pliable, but it is still green.

Fermentation turns the color. During fermentation, oxidation takes place and the tannin in tea changes chemically. It begins as a colorless, pungent substance. Gradually, as the tea ferments, the tannin turns red and loses its pungency. In the process, the tea gains flavor. The longer it ferments, the more its color grows, its pungency decreases, and its flavor increases. Pungency is not necessarily undesirable, but often, pungency and flavor are mutually exclusive. So the tea men monitor the fermentation carefully, turning to their experience

in striving for a tea that has either more pungency or greater flavor. The teas, spread out evenly on cement, tile, or glass surfaces, take their time. When they've turned a coppery red, the color of a new penny, fermentation is considered complete. This is the moment that must be preserved.

Firing does the job. Firing is essentially drying with hot-air machines, but it is not an indiscriminate blast of heat. It has to stop the fermenting by killing the bacteria and enzymes. But the temperature has to be modulated to dry the leaves without frying the outside and leaving the inside moist, in which case the tea will spoil. Like Goldilock's porridge, firing has to be just right or the tea's flavor will be compromised. At the end of firing, the tea is black.

Sorting is the final act. As the last step, the leaves are sifted so that they can be assembled according to size, an important factor in the types of teas they will become. The sizes are *whole leaf,* which are the largest and unbroken leaves; *broken* or *small leaf,* which may be torn pieces of leaf or smaller leaves; *fannings,* which are fragments; and *dust* or *fines,* even smaller fragments. As a measure of how precious tea is, consider that before machinery, dust was what remained to be swept up after preparing the leaves—and it was still valuable enough to sell.

BASIC BLACK

The only tea that undergoes the entire process described above is black tea. All black teas are fully fermented. This oxidation process alters the chemistry of the leaves so that the essential oils have an opportunity to develop. Because of this, most black teas will have greater pungency, which can also be described as astringency, or they may have fuller flavor or deeper color than green or oolong teas. None of these characteristics make black tea superior, just black.

DELICATE GREEN

Green tea is, of course, green, and it stays that way because the leaf undergoes a different process that prevents fermentation. There is no withering, but the leaves are steamed as soon as they are plucked. This whoosh of heat disarms the enzymes and essentially kills the leaf so fermentation is completely avoided. It also softens the leaf in preparation for rolling. In rolling, the flavorful juices are released and the tea attains its twist. The goal in making green tea is to rid the tea of moisture while holding on to the flavor and thus preserving it. To that end, the leaves are steamed and rolled repeatedly until all the moisture gradually evaporates and the leaves are crisp. Unlike black tea, the tannin in the leaves has not been altered so the tea remains green and all its pungency remains intact. Also unlike black tea, none of the essential oils that release flavor have been able to develop. So green tea has a pungency and delicacy all its own.

CHAMPAGNE OOLONG

Oolong, which is greenish brown tea, is thought of as the middle ground between black and green teas. However, this tea has a character of its own and deserves the respect of its original Chinese name, "black dragon." Oolong is semifermented, but the process is not merely a case of cutting the fermenting time. All the steps—withering, fermenting, rolling, and firing—are adjusted and abbreviated so that the leaves are captured and dried in a state that is not fully fermented. Most oolongs are produced in Taiwan (Formosa) today, although they originated in mainland China. Called the ''champagne of teas,'' oolongs are intensely piquant, perhaps because their leaves receive the least manipulation by man.

FRAGRANT POUCHONG

One more type of tea deserves mention and these are scented teas. The romance of jasmine or gardenia should not be overlooked. Any tea, black, green, or oolong, can be scented with flowers, like jasmine or gardenia. But to complicate things further, a tea that is not quite any of these is often used. That is *pouchong*, which is very close to green tea, but is allowed to rest a bit after plucking and is steamed just on the point of withering.

The gentleness of these, and most teas, belies the somewhat brutal process endured during their preparation. Having suffered through its ordeal, tea brings us the beauty of its transformation.

The Tea Trade: How Tea Is Sold

Why do they always put mud into coffee on board steamers?
Why does the tea generally taste of boiled boots?

—WILLIAM MAKEPEACE THACKERAY (1811–1863)

Never heard of Trincomalee? If you were a professional tea buyer you would. Trincomalee, in Sri Lanka, and its sister city, Columbo, are two of a handful of centers where tea auctions occur. It is there, not at your local supermarket, where the price of tea is set. Calcutta and Cochin in India, Jakarta and Medan in Indonesia, Nairobi and Mombassa in Kenya, Hamburg and Amsterdam in Europe, and, of course, London are among the few places where tea men gather as their wares get farther from the bush and closer to the cup.

SILENT AUCTIONS

Auctions are many-layered affairs with a phalanx of brokers, buyers, importers, and finally, retailers jockeying like horse traders for the finest tea at the most reasonable price. At any given point in the chain, competition rages over who will buy the best and to whom it will be sold. The actual moment of sale, however, is over in a flash, without any of the drama of art or antique auctions. All the work is done before. Professional tea buyers are well versed ahead of time on a tea's particulars—its district and garden, method of manufacture, unique characteristics, possible defects, and worth on the world market. They know practically everything about a tea except the name of the woman who plucked the leaves.

TONS OF TEA CHESTS

Faced with chests and chests of tea, they must be. A chest, made of plywood and lined with foil, weighs from 80 to 130 pounds, with "half" chests at 50 to 90 pounds. A small hole, bored in each one, offers samples to tea brokers. The auctioning is done in lots, usually of thirty to forty chests, but finer teas may be sold in lots of five or fewer. As in all commodities, there is always a small amount of the superior and large quantities of the ordinary. It is not an exaggeration to say that tons of tea are sold—five million pounds can change hands in a single day.

THE TEA TASTER

Someone has to test all that tea. Enter the tea taster, a man with a daunting task and one very sensitive palate. Anyone grappling with tea is up against the unpredictable, uncontrollable forces that all agricultural products face, not the least of which is weather. No tea from any single garden is ever necessarily the same as it was the year before; no natural commodity can be. Given variable conditions, no tea bush produces exactly the same leaf and bud year after year. Thus, nearly all teas are blends that strive to balance the differences in each year's crop so that consumers can count on consistent taste and quality. After all, tea drinkers expect Earl Grey to taste like Earl Grey, no matter how the bushes are buffeted by wind and rain or baked by the sun. It is the tea blender's job to make sure they are not disappointed.

The tea taster or blender performs this rather incredible balancing act with the skill of a man striding on a high wire. There is very little margin for error. In order to strike just the right combination of teas for a blend, he may have to assemble only a few teas or as many as thirty—possibly from four or five different countries—all in a state of seasonal flux. His only training can be experience, for no instruction could capture the variations in the ingredients. After perhaps seven years among the leaves, his talent for the art blossoms to the point where he can look at a tea and tell where it was grown and under what conditions, without even a taste.

THE TOUCH TEST

He begins with a handful. Tea leaves can reveal a great deal that has nothing to do with telling fortunes. Eyeing the leaves, the tea taster searches for the marks of quality. In black tea, for example, the color should be brownish black. A very dark black tea may be overbaked and burnt. The wither should be uniform. The leaves should be springy, not dry and crumbly. Teas that contain *tip,* the young shoots and buds, should show a golden hue, attained in the firing, and be long and well twisted. (However, some teas are never ''tippy'' and none the lesser for it.) The size should be uniform, but not necessarily large, and because tea engages all the senses, it should have an enticing aroma. If these criteria sound convoluted, it's only because they are. Rules are not written in stone; exceptions abound. What's the *best* tea? Only the tea blender knows for sure. His judgment is his guide, so the human factor may be the greatest variable of all.

THE TASTE TEST

This is certainly true of the tasting, which is *the* test. The tea taster must have an educated palate and a passion for his profession. How else can you explain a man who sloshes tea in his mouth, spits it out—and loves his work—to the point of being able to identify as many as 1,500 different teas? Tea tasting is serious business and is conducted as such with universally accepted procedures and standards of comparison. An exact amount of tea is brewed in a cup designed so that the tester can observe the leaves as they unfold and repose.

He inhales the steam of the brewing tea to appreciate the "nose." He observes the length of time the leaves take to infuse, and he examines the color of the liquor. In black tea, he hopes to find golden leaves, of even color; the more red, the richer the liquor; the more yellow, the greater the pungency. But if the leaves are green, they are underfermented and the tea will be bitter. In green tea, the leaves should be, naturally, green, and the liquor pale greenish gold, not brownish yellow. In oolong, green leaves with reddish brown edges are the ideal. In all cases, the liquid in the cup should be bright and clear.

The tea taster carries on like a wine taster without fear of intoxication. He slurps and sloshes and finally spits, all in the service of one of the most genteel pastimes man has ever devised. This may be abhorrent behavior for an afternoon tea party, but manners are not the point. The taster slurps a spoonful of tea, whooshing it to the back of his throat where the taste buds go to work and the nose gets a whiff of the tea's aroma. To cement his impression of a tea's character, he sloshes it around in his mouth, assessing its *flavor*, which is the taste and aroma; its *pungency*, which is its astringency or bite; and its *thickness*, which is its body or strength. A spittoon awaits. The taster spits. And in that moment, he notes everything he needs to know about that tea. At the end of the tasting session, he can choose which teas, in what proportions, he will use to create the blend he needs.

THE GOVERNMENT TEST

The tea tasters that have the last word about tea that is imported into the United States are members of the Board of Tea Experts and Tea Examiners, established by the Tea Act of 1897. Tea was probably the first commodity with an Act of Congress to protect consumers from substandard products. Operating under the Food and Drug Administration, six representatives from the tea industry and one government member set the minimum standards for acceptable tea in this country. Note that excellence is not their domain; rather it is their job to make sure that the tea is not terrible, contaminated, or impure. And they do so with considerable effort, for each year they are faced with a daunting number of teas to test. While the board maintains the lowest common denominator, it is up to consumers to improve the quality of tea imported into the United States by increasing the demand for the very best.

FINALE BY MACHINE

Tea companies have their own expert blenders, of course, and the proportions of teas they choose to create their brands are industrial-strength secrets. But once this very personal component of the tea process has occurred, human hands are off. Machines do the rest. Chests of tea are tipped into large drums, which do the bulk blending. The tea is then weighed by machine and packaged by machine. Loose tea in packages, tea bags in cardboard boxes, iced tea in jars, all are created by and conveyed through a mechanized leviathan until they emerge as the products you see on store shelves.

Tea, from seedling to aluminum can, is a microcosm of the merging of the Old World and New. Tea, as we know it, requires both the ancient practice of skilled hands pinching the first flush and the modern clamor of machinery. Tea is for all time.

Tea Territory: Tea-Growing Nations

INDIA

Nowhere has the cultivation of tea been more successful—and had such an inauspicious beginning—than in India. The tea bush grows wild in India, a gift of nature the British chose to ignore for years while their sights were set rigidly on China. Once they began cultivation, they did so wantonly, greedily, and for several years, ineffectually. Finally, in 1839, after twenty years of disregard and ineptitude, the London auction offered tea grown and produced in the gardens of India. The business of tea has never been the same.

Today, the English, tea's greatest advocates, import most of their tea from India, and not even half the country's output is exported. Tea has become the national drink of India. Each Indian consumes nearly a pound of tea a year on his own—in some concoctions that would astound their old colonial rulers. There are over 4,000 tea gardens in India, known by their garden "marks," a stencil of their name on their tea chests. Because of India's huge land mass and its topographical and climatic differences, India teas are judged first by the *region* and then by the altitude at which they are grown. Almost all teas are black and graded accordingly by size. Nearly all are worth knowing about.

Begin by dividing the country in half north and south, with three-quarters of the teas grown in the north.

One of the world's most admired teas is *Darjeeling,* grown in the shadow of the highest Himalayan mountains at altitudes that would leave sea-level humanity breathless. Here, at about 1,000 to close to 7,000 feet up, are bushes that grow tea leaves of every description—all of which produce a tea with a unique characteristic flavor. Climate, altitude, soil, and slow growth all contribute to the tea's greatness, but these factors also make harvesting difficult. Thus the crop is relatively small and very precious.

Northern India also encompasses the region of *Assam,* the largest tea growing area in the world, over two million acres in the northeastern valley of Brahmaputra. The first flush of its finest bushes produce leaves showing lovely tip, which are transformed into rich, pungent teas. Lakhimpur, Sibsagar, Darrang, and Nowgong are names associated with fine Assams. Assams are the basis of many British tea blends, but they can also stand alone. Along with Darjeeling, Assams are sold unblended, while all other India teas are found in blends.

Southern India's tea gardens are in the *Nilgiris Hills,* a name that means *Blue Mountain* for the blue mist that envelops the bushes on terraced slopes as high as 4,000 to 6,000 feet. Kanan Devan, Mundakayam, and Anaimalai are the names of notable teas from districts in these mountains where two monsoons annually drench the land with water and tea is produced year-round.

SRI LANKA

For close to twenty-five years, Ceylon, the island floating like a teardrop off the southern tip of India, has been called Sri Lanka. But its teas will forever be known as *Ceylons.* Welcome to some very fine teas, produced originally because, in 1869, a parasitic mushroom ravaged the island's coffee crop, then Ceylon's most important agricultural export. That year the plantation owners turned to tea and never looked back. The most famous tea marketer of all, Thomas Lipton (1850–1931), was the driving force behind the island's burgeoning industry. Although connoisseurs may cringe, the name Lipton is still synonymous with tea.

All Ceylon black teas are characterized, not so much by district but by altitude, as in *high grown,* over 4,000 feet; *medium grown,* 2,000 to 4,000 feet; and *low grown,* below 2,000 feet. As might be expected, the lower grown teas are plain and best for blends and the quality is more or less commensurate with altitude. The districts themselves are not as important an indicator of quality with the exception of a few such as Nuwara Eliya, Uva, and Dimbula. However, the weather in any given year will also affect the outcome. These teas are softer, not as pungent as Indian teas, and most often sold as part of blends.

INDONESIA

The tea in your cup may very well be partly Indonesian, but only the importer knows for sure. Indonesian tea is found virtually only in blends—good, serviceable blends, but hardly distinguished ones. But in the marketing of tea, usefulness is good business, and Indonesia is the fourth largest tea producing country in the world. These teas are grown either in Java or Sumatra and carry the names of those islands. The bulk is produced in Java, a label more readily associated with coffee, which is also grown in this archipelago. Shopping for tea, you will not be confronted with an Indonesian choice, but the likelihood is that a blend you buy may contain a high grown tea from the mountains of Java.

TAIWAN

Tea, an ancient art, refuses to relinquish its nomenclature to modernity. There is no Taiwan tea, only Formosa tea. The fact that Formosa is now called Taiwan is irrelevant to tea people; only the land matters. And the soil on this Chinese island outpost is perfect for oolong. Formosa oolong, grown *not* on high ground, but in richly nutrient lowlands, began as a substitute for tea from mainland China. But nature, ever rebellious against predictability, produced a leaf so superior for oolong that the semifermented tea is now virtually defined by Taiwan. These teas are known for their unusual character, for their pungency, flavor, and sparkling amber liquor. And they are known as Formosa Oolong.

The people of Taiwan also produce other teas that are derived from their Chinese origins. Their black teas are Keemun types and Lapsang, the tea with the smoky flavor. In Taiwan, the smokiness is the result of curing rather than from the soil, as it is on the mainland. The country exports green tea, sold as Special Chun Mee, Chun Mee, Sow Mee, and Gunpowder. Pouchong, the scented oolong, is also produced in Taiwan, and jasmine, the floral that brings us the aroma of the East, is the one most likely to be found in the West.

CHINA

The next time someone says he wouldn't act differently for all the tea in China, give up the fight. His position is entrenched, his resolve is beyond firm, his decision implacable, and he cannot be convinced otherwise. All the tea in China is *a lot*. Not as much as it used to be, but still a great deal. What is amazing about China's tea output is not the quantity, but the number of varieties. To classify the teas just by geography is staggering, and that doesn't include the quality of the leaves or the manufacturing. China is a huge land mass covered by tea grown in small patches and, for the sake of general classification, geography is the most practical guide. The country produces black (called red in China), green, oolong, white, and brick teas.

Black Teas (Hong Cha) are divided along a north/south

axis and *Congou,* a term that refers to the manufacturing process, is the word to remember. North China Congous include one of the most famous teas in the world, Keemuns, full-flavored, thick-bodied teas. Other noteworthy teas, such as Ningchows and Ichangs are also produced in this area. If musical analogies could be used to categorize teas, North China Congous would strike a bass tone, while South China Congous would sound more like a clarinet, a higher, brighter note. Among these, grown in the Fukien province, are Paklums, Padraes, and Ching Wos. The famous, smoky tasting Lapsang Souchongs are also produced in the south.

China Green Teas (Lu Cha) must be discussed in terms of geography *and* style. There are three areas, *country greens,* all the green teas in China except for those originating in the areas around the cities Hoochow and Pingsuey, which are in Chekiang province. Moyens and Tienkais are the finest of the country greens, teas with enough flavor and body to surprise many a devoted black tea drinker. Ever since an English sailor mistook China green tea for ammunition, *Gunpowder* has been the most recognizable type. A variation on Gunpowder, but not as fine, is Imperial. And *Young Hyson* (new leaf) and *Hyson* (older leaf) are the two other most common China greens. Once these pedestrian names for tea types are acknowledged, it is far more pleasant to contemplate the lovely, whimsical names that the Chinese give their green tea like Snow Dragon and Spring Plums.

China White Tea is a case of true exclusivity. A very small spot on the planet produces the tea bush from which it comes, and these are almost all in the Fukien Province. White tea is distinguished by what it is *not*—neither fermented nor rolled.

China oolongs can only be mentioned in a negative comparison with Formosa oolong—there is no comparison. And China brick tea is listed only for its novelty, not its taste. Made primarily from the remains of the black tea process, a brick is six pounds of tea compressed into a solid rectangle, a weighty demonstration of quantity over quality.

Also along geographical lines, China teas are often named for the province of their origin or the port from which they were shipped. Thus, Guangdongs are teas from the province of that name. And any tea that left China from Canton (now Guangzhou), Foochow, or Shanghai could carry that name right to your cup.

JAPAN

There are more McDonald's in Japan than anywhere else outside the United States. And more green tea. That may seem incongruous, but not to the Japanese. In Japan, green tea goes with everything. The third largest tea producer in the world, after India and Sri Lanka, Japan only exports a fraction of its crop; in fact, the country *imports* tea to satisfy its unquenchable thirst. All of it is green.

But not all green tea is created equal. The Japanese match the leaf with various manufacturing processes and produce both outstanding and ordinary teas. When they begin with the best leaf, they create Gyokuro tea or Pearl Dew. Grown in the area of Yamashiro near Kyoto, this special tea is coddled beneath sun shelters as it matures. Only the tenderest buds are used and these are hand rolled. When these leaves are not rolled but naturally dried as flat leaf, they are called Tencha and they become the powder that is used in the Japanese tea ceremony. So particular is this tea that the leaves are separated into usucha, blue green leaves that make a thin, light colored tea, and koicha, dark green leaves that make a dark, thick tea.

Most Japanese, and the rest of us who enjoy subtle and astringent Japanese greens, drink sencha, rather misnamed ordinary tea, an umbrella category for many very fine teas made with young leaves and manufactured in a variety of ways. They are refired before export to ensure that all moisture is eliminated and are often classified according to this final blast of heat. Thus, green tea from Japan may be called *pan-fired,* a well-twisted tea polished by metal-conducted heat. Guri is the curliest of the pan-fired teas. *Basket-fired* are longer leaves, nicely twisted and heated in baskets. And *natural leaf* is either pan-fired or basket-fired, but coarser leaf of undependable quality. Finally, there is bancha, which is made from older-growth leaves plucked late in the season. This is the Japanese everyday tea, low in caffeine and inexpensive, not representative of the country's finest, but widely used.

There would be tea to drink in the world without Japan, of course, but there would be no tea culture. The Chinese originated the tea ceremony, but the Japanese raised it to the level of transcendent art. The ancient way of Japanese tea was life lived in the realm of painting, architecture, flower arranging, and landscaping. It was a guiding philosophy that celebrated the universal in the everyday—in tea. Japan is as important to tea as the leaf itself.

KENYA

Kenya is blessed with a high volcanic mountain, Mount Kenya, and good rainfall, offering tea what it needs to thrive: altitude, rich soil, and moisture. This is a successful country at growing tea, exporting a great deal to the United States and England. At this time, most of that product finds its way into ordinary tea bags, but there is hope that more distinguished teas will be forthcoming. Other countries in East Africa also grow tea on their mountain slopes but with less success.

TURKEY

While the words *Turkish* and *coffee* blend in the mind better than *Turkey* and *tea,* the country does grow its own and drinks nearly all of it. Called *çay,* Turkish tea is black and distinctively different. Unfortunately, a trip to Istanbul is the best way to try it.

EAST AND SOUTHEAST ASIA

Bangladesh and Nepal, neighbors of India, share some tea growing territory. Iran has estates of its own. And Vietnam is resurrecting its historic tea growing capacity. It is a work in progress and one worth looking forward to.

Centuries of
Tea

Graciousness, Greed, and Gunfire: The History of Tea

There is much of mystery, poetry, and romance in the march of tea down through the years.

—WILLIAM UKERS,
THE ROMANCE OF TEA, 1936

The Bible begins with the creation of Heaven and Earth, but there is no reference to tea. Perhaps the Creator was too busy to mention it that first action-packed week. Certainly, there must have been a tea bush in the Garden of Eden because that's where it belonged. To much of the world, tea has been paradise in a cup—at least since 2737 B.C.

THE FIRST SIP AND THE LAST WORD

That was the first year the tea leaf met boiling water—and in very good company. According to legend, Emperor Shen Nung, scion of the gods and early health zealot known as the Divine Healer, was boiling water for drinking when the wind swept a leaf from a branch into his water. The aroma of the infusion wafted to his nostrils. The drink enthralled him. Writings attributed to the emperor claimed tea to be medicinal and delicious, thirst quenching, refreshing, cheering, and healing. Man's yearning for such a potion seems to be eternal.

But written history is not. Subsequent claims and even political revisionism disputed Shen Nung's authorship and works that purported to mention tea over the next two centuries were cast in doubt. Historians have settled on a dictionary compiled by a Chinese folk hero, the Duke of Chou, in the twelfth century B.C. and annotated in A.D. 350 by Kuo P'u as the first reliably written description of tea. "The plant is small like the gardenia, sending forth its leaves even in the winter," Kuo P'u wrote. Tea was on the books.

But not its name. Chinese ideographs, inscrutable to the West like so much of the East, make the origins of the word *tea* nearly untranslatable. But by the eighth century A.D., the Chinese words in use were *ch'a,* pronounced *cha* in Cantonese and *t'e,* pronounced *tay* in the dialect of the province of Amoy. The linguistic pattern was set. Commerce brought the word and the commodity into other languages. Part of the world, including India and Turkey, still use derivatives of *ch'a,* while the English followed the Dutch who made *thee* out of *t'e. Tay,* the first English pronunciation, evolved into the perfect cup of *tea.*

CHINA: THE CLASSIC OF TEA

But tea was not there yet. Chinese history, a firestorm of bloody upheavals interspersed with periods of elegant philosophy and inspiring beauty, swept the development of tea along with it. The fourth century saw tea made as medicine, bitter but said to be effective in curing everything from mental to physical distresses. In the fifth century, tea propagation began, and tea appeared in ledgers as a trading commodity. As a matter of fact, among China's rural population, tea was used as currency very early in its history. By the sixth century, tea came out of the medicine chest and into the parlor, outgrowing its medicinal reputation and becoming a refreshment. In another hundred years, the demand increased, farmers recognized the profits to be made in tea, and cultivation became widespread. Tea took hold.

The seventh century approached, and tea entered three great periods of development and transformation: The T'ang

Dynasty (618–907), known as the Classic period of tea, the Sung Dynasty (690–1280), the Romantic period, and the Ming Dynasty (1368–1644), the Naturalistic period. In other words, tea made history.

And Lu Yü was the agent. Here was a man with a kaleidoscopic career—orphan, recluse, circus performer, and scholar—who essentially was recruited by the emerging tea industry in A.D. 780 to write a book that would help spread the popularity of tea. His work, *Ch'a Ching* or *The Classic of Tea*, turned out to be a marketing man's dream. But it was more than that. The book became an expression of the ideals of the T'ang Dynasty, a period in which the beliefs of China's three major philosophies and religions, Confucianism, Buddhism, and Taoism, found common ground in celebrating life in each moment of existence. The *Tao*, or the *Way,* found harmony, beauty, and order in the ordinary tasks of life. And through *Ch'a Ching*, the ritual of tea preparation and tea drinking became the symbol of this philosophy.

Lu Yü divides his book into three volumes in which he patiently, deliberately, and very specifically instructs readers in all the aspects of tea: poetic descriptions of the leaves, instructions regarding the boiling of the water, a detailing of the implements used, and precepts on how to drink the tea. Improbable as it may seem, Lu Yü so perfectly captured the essence of the T'ang Dynasty that classical Chinese art and philosophy became forever wedded with the rituals of tea. History would change tea in China, but time never erased this ideal.

To Lu Yü, tea was symbolic, a representation of the universal in the particular, of the divine in everyday life, but in the era of the Sung, tea became a pleasure unto itself. And the leaves that Lu Yü so lyrically described never made it to the cup but were ground to a fine powder and then whisked into boiling water. The territory of tea broadened into the general culture where tea contests were held to extol new varieties, tea houses inspired architecture and landscaping, and tea bowls were created especially for tasting. Zen Buddhists took up tea and developed the tea rituals that became the forerunner of the Japanese tea ceremony. Teas were given fanciful names like *sparrow's tongue* and *ear of corn,* for the poetical permeated all facets of the culture. The Sung were a romantic people.

The Mongols were not. When they invaded, trouncing the country with the heavy boots of their leader, Kublai Khan, tea suffered a hundred-year setback. When finally the Ming dynasty reunited China, tea reappeared in a more egalitarian form. Whipped tea, exotic and cumbersome to prepare, disappeared in favor of steeped leaves. The middle class took the reins of society and tea became an everyday occurrence stripped of its exotic aura. Ming porcelain bowls, white lively patterns, showed off tea's liquor instead of the serious ceramics of tea's Classical and Romantic eras. This was the Naturalistic period in which tea came into the kitchen, enjoyed by everyone for its flavor and aroma, but worshipped by few. That was 350 years ago. Today, people all over the world

embrace tea as if it has always been their national drink. It has not. Tea is forever indelibly Chinese.

JAPAN: THE ART OF TEA

Only the Japanese can come close to claiming tea as their own. It was they who refined what they learned from the Chinese and elevated the tea ceremony to an exalted position in their culture. Their impetus was primarily Zen Buddhist. Indeed, the prevailing Japanese myth on the origin of tea involves Bodhidharma or Daruma, Indian saint and patriarch of Japanese Zen Buddhism. According to the legend, Daruma traveled from India to China where he endeavored to meditate, uninterrupted, for nine years. Unfortunately and evidently unforgivably, sleep overcame him several years into this superhuman effort. Disgusted, he sliced off his betraying eyelids and cast them on the ground, whereupon the tea bush sprang to life, bearing with it the drink of eternal refreshment. The harshness of this drama is some indication of the seriousness with which the Japanese took their tea.

Japanese monks who traveled to China for immersion in Buddhism brought back tea as early as the eighth century, but in the twelfth century, a monk named Eisai offered the cup of tea that has kept Japanese kettles boiling for hundreds of years. He wrote the *Book of Tea Sanitation*, extolling the drink's virtues. Then he very publicly and miraculously cured a severely ailing government official with a sip of his personal brew. A mass conversion to tea spread through the empire. Japan was hooked.

But men, of course, are not as pure as tea. The violent thrashings of governmental changes and their subsequent societal upheavals over the next few centuries naturally influenced and ultimately dissipated the culture of tea in Japan. Yet, the monks remained steadfast in their pursuit of tea, integrating it into their contemplation of the universe. Gradually, meandering through the philosophical gardens of Taoism and Zen, they came to Teaism and its epitome, the Japanese Tea Ceremony. In his historic work, *The Book of Tea*, Okakura Kakuzo, a twentieth-century scholar, describes Teaism as a religion of aestheticism. Kakuzo defines Teaism as a practice that requires rigorous intellectual devotion, "a cult founded on the adoration of the beautiful among the sordid facts of everyday existence. It inculcates purity and harmony, the mystery of mutual charity, the romanticism of the social order." And, he wrote, "It is essentially a worship of the Imperfect, as it is a tender attempt to accomplish something possible in this impossible thing we know as life." Thus, the Tea Ceremony, called *Chanoyu*, became so much more than a cup of tea.

By the sixteenth century, the Tea Ceremony embraced art, landscaping, and architecture. Tea rooms and tea gardens were built specifically to be in harmony with nature and the Zen concept of tea. All tea's disciples were, Kakuzo wrote, "aristocrats in taste," and chief among them were the rigorously trained tea masters, who, the author explains, fostered the greatest achievements in Japanese pottery, painting, and textiles and even influenced the conduct of life, encouraging humility, morality, and an appreciation of beauty and simplicity.

The man of Japan's finest tea hour was Rikyu, tea master to the Emperor Hideyoshi in 1588. He streamlined the ceremony, honing it to its most exquisitely austere essentials, a ceremony of purity and beauty, politeness and harmony. His precepts about the room arrangements, floral accompaniments, clothing, equipment, order of events, and tea preparation have endured until today. In contemporary Japan, tea is still the drink of the many, but only the few practice the revered art of *Chanoyu.*

The Japanese, who were never receptive to Western barbarians, would have been appalled to see how the English

aristocracy first took their tea. They slurped it from saucers. It wasn't pretty, but it was a beginning. Eventually, England's mercantile thrust into the Far East in the seventeenth century would bring tea to the Western world. But in the race for trade in the Orient, the Portuguese got there first and then the Dutch, who in 1610 were the first to bring Chinese and Japanese teas to Europe. The English had to hustle, so they established an empire.

ENGLAND: USURPER OF TEA

The history of tea in England encompasses everything that can happen to a nation in three centuries: political changes, wars, social upheavals, religious divisions, economic disasters and triumphs, and cultural transitions. Tea was at the heart of these transformations. The agent of many of these changes was the British East India Company, established in 1600, to which the government gave a monopoly on trade in the East Indies. In this pursuit, the John Company, as it became known, could wage war, annex territory, make laws, coin British currency, and, in essence, execute the powers of England wherever it put its foot down in the East.

By 1700, the company had outstripped competition from the Dutch and Portuguese, clamped an iron grip on India, and achieved more than a foothold in trade with China, ever a reluctant and suspicious partner. Tea was supplanting coffee as the beverage of choice in England, and the British East India Company knew its fortunes lay in an ever greater supply.

During the seventeenth century, while ruthless business a half a world a way kept queens and commoners enthralled with afternoon tea, the John Company thrived. But the eighteenth century brought economic problems for England and some political difficulties that involved the prophetic Boston Tea Party. The world was changing, and oppressive taxation, restrictive trading practices, and dictatorial government, the circumstances under which the John Company thrived, were severely challenged at the end of the eighteenth century. Under pressure from tea merchants led by Richard Twining, a tea name to reckon with, the British government rescinded the company's monopoly in 1813. But greed does not die quietly.

One of the reasons for the dire financial straits of England and the John Company was China's insistence on currency as payment for tea rather than trading for other commodities. To rectify this uneven balance of trade, English merchants made the Chinese common man an illegal offer he could not refuse: opium. Grown in India under English control, poppies were plentiful. Opium addiction was not new to the Chinese, but greater availability increased demand and, as addictions do, this one widened its pernicious grip. Tensions between the Chinese government, attempting to hold back the plague, and the British East India Company finally inflamed to the point of armed conflict. The Opium War (1840–1842) was not a sterling moment in English history. Easily defeated, the Chinese were forced to open more ports for trading. But by this time, even though England was consuming an insatiable thirty million pounds of tea, the John Company had been stripped of its monopoly and succumbed to competition.

The Americans were supplying it. The upstart colony across the Atlantic joined the tea trade by building a better mousetrap, the clipper ship. It's a long way from Foochow to London, and in the 1800s, ships were the only way to get there. When the Americans first began trade with China in conventional ships, the English were not concerned, but when the first clipper ships flew the distance in record-breaking time, they knew they were in trouble. Sleek, streamlined, needle thin, and top-heavy with sails, the clippers were the glamour girls of the ocean. And they could move.

England quickly built her own and, aside from commerce, the beauty of these ships inspired some of best sport racing in sailing history. In the 1850s and 1860s, clippers swept around the world in tea races between London and Foochow, adding romance and drama to the modern history of tea. But the era of the British monopoly in China was finally over, and the English were forced to search elsewhere for tea. They found it in India, right under their noses.

INDIA AND CEYLON: THE BREADBASKETS OF TEA

India came late to the game of tea under the stewardship of the English colonial empire. The indigenous Indian tea plant was ignored by England for many years as the British rather blindly focused on tea in China. It took a Scotsman, Major Robert Bruce, to recognize it and, after he died, his brother, to wrestle with establishing productive tea gardens. At last, in 1839, when native Indian tea was presented at auction in London, the world took it seriously—very seriously. Still, another thirty years passed before the industry overcame inept management, poor labor, and hustlers with the equivalent of a gold rush mentality.

In the end, tea lovers benefited the most. The two main tea

growing regions of the country, Assam and Darjeeling, are synonymous with great teas. Primarily black teas are produced in India, and nobody does it better. India's neighbor, Sri Lanka, which sells tea by its original name, Ceylon, is also a latecomer to the industry with a fine reputation. Only after its coffee crop was blighted did Sri Lanka begin growing tea and that was in the 1880s. Thomas Lipton, of tea fame, jump-started the tea gardens there and they have been successful ever since. Without tea from India and Sri Lanka, the West would be very thirsty for tea indeed.

India does not have the ancient tea traditions of China and Japan, and the purity of tea has never been an ideal in India. In a country where *chai* is hawked on roadsides and railway stations, where tea is deliciously concocted with milk and sugar and spices, tea in India has always been motivated by profit and pleasure. That isn't to say the Indians don't understand fine tea—they produce the largest crop and some of the best in the world.

And the world is grateful. Today, China and Japan, the two countries who have contributed the most to what we know about tea, consume most of their own production. Ceylon and India, along with Indonesia, Kenya, and others make it possible for the rest of us to enjoy a communal cup of tea, knowing that all over the globe people are doing the same.

From Coffeehouse to Tea Table: Tea in England

The progress of this famous plant has been something like the progress of truth; suspected at first, though very palatable to those who had courage to taste it; resisted as it encroached; abused as its popularity seemed to spread; and establishing its triumph at last, in cheering the whole land from the palace to the cottage, only by the slow and restless efforts of time and its own virtues.

—ISAAC D'ISRAELI (1766–1848)

It may be hard to believe, but tea in England began in coffeehouses. In the mid-1600s, London alone was home to at least 2,000 dimly lit, tobacco-filled establishments that catered exclusively to men, talking mostly of politics. Artists, men of letters, military types, clergymen, merchants, physicians, and others congregated in collegial groups and wrestled opinions over coffee. Until tea came along.

TEA: PRO AND CON

In 1660, entrepreneurial coffeehouse owner Thomas Garway was the first to encourage customers to try the exotic brew. He reported that the "Leaf is of such known vertues, that those very Nations famous for Antiquity, Knowledge, and

Wisdom, do frequently sell it among themselves.'' And he was absolutely not shy about touting its health benefits, declaring it to be ''most wholesome, preserving in perfect health until extreme Old Age.''

Not everyone agreed. Tea had already been introduced in Europe, and while the Dutch, the first importers, had found it agreeable, the Germans and French raged a battle over its curative or deleterious effects. An appalled German doctor insisted, in 1635, that ''It hastens the death of those who drink it, especially if they have passed the age of forty years.'' In direct contradiction, an eighty-one-year-old Dutch physician presented himself as living proof that ''those who use it are for that reason alone exempt from all maladies and reach an extreme old age.'' Unlikely as it seems, there were Englishmen who continued to find tea a nasty habit even after it had been in the country for a hundred years.

PRINCESS OF TEA

It took a woman to point the way. The Portuguese Princess Catherine de Braganza married Charles II in 1662. Included in her trousseau, which must have been considerable, was tea, already a favorite of the Portuguese nobility. The English court gentility followed her lead and Edmund Waller, a poet, even wrote a poem in praise of tea and the new queen on her birthday. Only part of it follows, for the whole is, unfortunately, more of the same:

> *The Muse's friend, Tea, does our fancy aid,*
> *Repress those vapours which the head invade,*
> *And keep that palace of the soul serene,*
> *Fit on her birthday to salute the Queen.*

Catherine was a little ahead of her time. The British East India Company imported its first small cargo of tea into England in 1669, and regular shipments didn't take place until several years later. But tea was catching on with the people who could afford it, and they had to be very rich indeed. Tea was heavily taxed then, and its expense gave it a certain ca-

chet among the wealthy. What is rare becomes valuable and to own something valuable becomes a matter of pride. Tea became a trophy of the rich.

And Thomas Twining (yes, *that* Twining) capitalized on the age-old art of conspicuous consumption. In 1714, he bought a coffeehouse, changed its name to the Golden Lyon and sold tea to both men and *women*. In no time, the sale of tea outstripped the sale of coffee, and a tea empire was born. Today, Samuel Twining is the ninth generation chairman of Twinings Tea Company of England—all because his ancestor had the acumen to know that women will covet and pay dearly for what is fashionable. Tea became big business.

TOTAL TEA

In the eighteenth century, tea suffered the consequences of a commodity on which a country depends. Its price fluctuated according to politics and economics. Its taxes were raised and repealed; it was adulterated and smuggled. But most importantly, it traveled out of the royal courts and into the homes of ordinary Englishmen, whose oftentimes meager repasts depended on tea for refreshment and sustenance. How one took one's tea became a matter of social class and breeding, but every Englishman took tea. Life without tea was no longer acceptable.

GARDENS OF TEA

In the second half of the eighteenth century, coffeehouses fell into disrepute, and tea moved out into gardens, where both men and women could mingle more agreeably, where, in fact, the "best" people went for recreation. The grandest and most famous tea gardens, like the Vauxhall and Ranelagh, entertained ladies and gentlemen with dancing, bowling greens, concerts, and even gambling and racing. At the center was tea, "the Elegant Regale of Tea, Coffee, and Bread and Butter," served amid thousands of twinkling candle lanterns, the swishing of elegant skirts, and the tipping of top hats. A place to see and be seen, tea gardens were more than a picnic.

TEA TIMES

Tea gardens are a memory now, but afternoon tea is an institution. Though the custom probably began in the seventeenth century with the wealthy and their newfound Oriental passion, legend has it that the practice was established in the early nineteenth century by the honest, healthy appetite of Anna, Duchess of York (1783–1857). At that time, lunch was a light meal and dinner was served as late as nine P.M. in more elegant households. Anna, bless her, got *hungry* in the late afternoon, and to counteract what she called a "sinking feeling," she called for tea, oh, and tarts, and cakes, and biscuits, and, perhaps, a bit of bread and butter and cheesecake.

The English have never been the same. Victorian women embraced the idea and perpetuated the ritual with such devotion that afternoon tea has become symbolic of England's civilizing influence in the world. Being "at home" for tea and making calls for tea were more than an idle pastime. *De rigueur* social networking took place over teacups and cucumber sandwiches. Today, daily afternoon tea is a victim of hectic modern schedules, but people still entertain with afternoon tea, and many hotels and inns offer a whiff of its former grandeur. If one is lucky enough to be at the Peninsula Hotel in Hong Kong, the Plaza in New York, or the Ritz in London, it is still possible to enjoy a very regal, exceptionally lovely, classically English afternoon tea.

If afternoon tea seems like an indulgence of the upper classes, it was. Not everyone had the leisure to sip tea from china cups, nibble on dainty sandwiches with a wisp of filling, and raise eyebrows over a new tidbit of gossip. Working people worked during the hour of afternoon tea. Their tea came later, was really supper, and came to be called high tea. At about six o'clock, the man of the house returned from work to find the table laid with an egg dish or cold meat and vegetables, bread and scones, and tea. Out of necessity, the meal was not elaborate, but tea was the one necessity.

TEA ON THE MOVE

Tea went on the move in the second half of the nineteenth century, onto trains and railway stations and later onto planes, so that no traveling Englishman would be without tea. Tea shops, the oasis of refreshment for ordinary Englishwomen,

came into being when the female manager of a branch of the ABC, the Associated Bread Company, pulled up a couple of chairs in the back room for tea with friends. The idea was so popular that ABCs became the McDonald's of the tea trade, filling a need that no one had recognized before.

Certainly, few would have anticipated that tea and dancing would become partners, but they did at the turn of the century when the Edwardian period under Edward VIII became the Gay Nineties. The cheerfully elegant, rather decadent *thé dansant* was born in France and imported to England. To make the combination even less plausible, the dance of the hour was the *tango*. Picture the sexy, sultry tango and formal, decorous tea, an odd couple to be sure, but perhaps just the right mix to make life interesting on a late and dreary London afternoon.

From the moment the English came to tea, they used it to

cheer their afternoons, shore up their social lives, relieve boredom, stimulate conversation, soothe suffering, comfort sorrow, refresh their energies, and revive their souls. The English never imbued tea with philosophy as the Chinese did, or raised its preparation to an art form like the Japanese. The British adopted it as if it had been a missing element in their national identity. Tea, which began as a purely mercantile venture, became one of the defining cultural characteristics of what it means to be English.

The Boston Tea Party Continues: Tea in America

> The waters in the rebel bay
> Have kept the tea-leaf savor;
> Our old North-Enders in their spray
> Still taste a Hyson flavor;
> And freedom's teacup still o'erflows
> With ever-fresh libations
> To cheat of slumber all her foes
> And cheer the wakening nations!
>
> —OLIVER WENDELL HOLMES
> (1809–1894), "BALLAD OF
> THE BOSTON TEA PARTY"

Picture tea: lovely, hot, and soothing. And war. *War?* Yes, remember the Boston Tea Party, taxation without representation, and, of course, Patrick Henry's spitfire call to arms, "Give me liberty or give me death!" Now *that's* war, and tea was part of it. Certainly, as Jamie Shalleck says in the book, *Tea*, "the American Revolution was not fought *for* tea, but it was fought *over* tea." Tea was the flash point, the spark that ignited the Colonial fire that burned the bridge with England.

DUTCH TREAT

Actually, it was not the English but the Dutch who brought tea to America. Settled in New Amsterdam (which later became New York), Dutch women set out to create an aristocracy all their own in the New World. Tea was the drink of Holland's upper class in the middle of the seventeenth century, and so it was tea they brought with them. Elaborate tea services crossed the Atlantic, complete with teapots, hot water pots, bite and stir boxes (which held lumps of sugar to nibble on and powdered sugar to stir), tongs, strainers, silver spoons, cups, and saucers. For an afternoon tea, seriously gracious hostesses served not one, but perhaps three types of tea to satisfy their guests. Being socially correct always did require paraphernalia.

TEA MEN AND TEA WATER

When the English took the territory in 1674, they naturally elaborated on the rituals of tea. By the 1700s, Tea Gardens, an idea brought from *their* Old World antecedents, sprouted up on the outskirts of the city. Here natural springs provided the best water possible, and entertainments, fireworks, and band concerts amused both ladies and gentlemen. When people couldn't get to the water, the water came to them, pumped into barrels and sold from carts by Tea Men all over town. Imagine Manhattan as a place where vendors shouted "Tea water! Come out and get your tea water!"

TEA LADIES

Meanwhile, delight in tea spread to Boston, where ladies called upon one another for afternoon tea with a singular social twist—each brought her own cup, saucer, and teaspoon. Tea drinking spawned an industry, setting trends in silverware for tea services, in stoneware and porcelain designs for teapots, and in styles of furniture—one had to have, at the very least, one tea table. Tea became a patron of the arts. Teapots were being made by Paul Revere long before he galloped

through the night into the mythology of American history. By the middle of the 1700s, tea drinking was so popular and so much a part of the social fabric of the colonies that nothing short of war could have torn the ladies from their tea. And it did.

TEA TAX

The business of tea became enmeshed in the business of politics which, as always, took its cues from those diabolical twins, money and power. The story of how the world of England and its American colonies came to turn on a tea leaf involves both. In the 1770s, the East India Company, Britain's huge monopoly, was in financial trouble and turned to its government for help in marketing tea to America. At the same time, the coffers of Great Britain's treasury were depleted by skirmishes with the French. The country needed revenue and also wanted to tighten its reign over the colonies. However, at the same time, spirited Americans were developing an itch for independence. A collision course was set, and tea became the turn in the road where the crash occurred.

Without heeding the warning signs, George III and his chancellor of the exchequer began imposing new taxes on the colonies. They met resistance and, at first, retreated. Their final misguided move was the Tea Act of 1773, which called for a modest tax on tea, and, in essence, gave the East India Company a monopoly on its sales in America. But the growing Colonial merchant class, with an eye toward its own economic self-interest, viewed the decree as a double offense— taxation without representation *and* restraint of free trade.

THE TEA PARTY

The English made a further mistake by miscalculating that the American woman, in her desire for tea, would have a restraining influence on the more radical men among them. They were wrong. Women from Boston to Washington banished tea from the table. And the men threw it overboard. When the East India Company's ships landed in Boston loaded with tea, fifty men disguised as Indians, dumped 342 chests of tea into the sea. The British branded them outlaws; Americans honored them as the first patriots of the Revolutionary War and called the event the Boston Tea Party.

FORTUNES IN TEA

As might be expected, tea drinking as an American pastime plunged along with the tea leaves in the harbor. It has never completely recovered. That is not to say that American businessmen lost interest in tea. Indeed, in the 1800s, the first Americans to become millionaires, when being a millionaire was inestimably wealthy, found fortunes in tea. Thomas Perkins, scion of a patrician Boston family, traded directly with China. A man of his word, whose reputation was impeccable, Perkins was so trusted by the Chinese that he built an empire without ever signing a contract. John Jacob Astor amassed his first fortune in furs and then traded them to China for tea and made even more money.

One house of money that tea built in the nineteenth century blossomed in the twentieth century as the A & P supermarkets. The company began as the Great American Tea Company, a mail-order business, and developed into the Great Atlantic and Pacific Tea Company. Their wagon routes brought tea, coffee, and spices to settlers as they pushed the frontier, and the country, to the West Coast. The Grand Union food store chain, which began in 1872 as a tea company, still stands as a sentinel in the suburbs to remind us of those early enterprises and their astounding success.

DANCING TO TEA

But tea drinking, as an American pastime, had to wait until another social phenomenon swept it back into popularity; this time it was "tea dances." Once again, the classes with the leisure time to indulge themselves led the way. In the late 1800s, afternoon tea service began to appear in elegant hotels. Again, tea gained ground among the privileged few. By 1910, hotels found a way to mix tea and company and capitalize on a trend that was sweeping the country: daytime dancing. One dance craze followed the next: the maxie, the turkey trot, the bunny hug; scandalous dances in which partners moved oh-so-close to one another gave dancing a racy and delicious cachet. Hotels became the venues where people rushed to dance the castle walk, the shimmy, and the tango, sexy even in the afternoon. Tea was served and the name *tea dances* stuck—along with a renewed interest in the drink.

ICED, BAGGED, AND INSTANT

About that time, America introduced the nation's dubious contributions to the art of tea drinking: iced tea, tea bags, and instant tea, three formulations that have never warmed the hearts of serious tea drinkers. Iced tea is one of those products that sprang into being when improvisation became the mother of invention. It was 1904, it was the St. Louis World's Fair, and it was hot, too hot for tea. Richard Blechynden, representative of tea plantations in India, came to the event to promote his teas. Not surprisingly, giving away hot tea in stifling weather was a lot like offering ice in winter. Savvy entrepreneur that he was, Blechynden got hold of some ice, added it to his tea, and handed it out to perspiring fairgoers. Bingo. America's favorite summertime drink was born.

Tea bags were an accidental discovery, too, but theirs was a case of mistaken identity. In a money-saving maneuver, a tea importer named Thomas Sullivan tried sending out samples of tea to customers in little silk bags, rather than tins, which required more tea. The retailers mistakenly brewed the tea in the bags and immediately requested more—bags, that is. It became apparent that they could sell all kinds of tea in these premeasured, self-straining little pouches. Eventually, all America warmed to the idea of not having to measure tea and deal with leftover leaves. The tea bag took over.

Instant tea took an evolutionary route, developing along with technology, and the drink didn't really become palatable or popular until the 1950s. The powder in the instant tea jar is produced by brewing tea leaves, extracting the liquid, and adding preservatives and sometimes flavorings and sugar or sweetener. Spooned into a glass or jug, dissolved in water and ice, the drink is as common as air conditioners whenever the temperature rises. Now iced tea, presweetened and flavored, has made the ultimate leap from brewing into the realm of the almost-soft-drink market—tea in cans and bottles. The bottles aim for chic with designer shapes and labels and protestations of natural products. If the way they are being snapped up is a harbinger of the future, America is once again close to becoming a tea drinking nation.

The Types
of Tea

Orange Pekoe Is Not a Fruit: Tea Grades

Its proper use is to amuse the idle, and relax the studious, and dilute the full meals of those who cannot use exercise, and will not use abstinence.

—SAMUEL JOHNSON (1709–1784)

In a world as attuned to fine distinctions as that of tea, there are bound to be standards. Unfortunately, the nomenclature for categories has come to us sifted over so much time and through so many cultures that we are left with more confusion than clarity. Do not be daunted. The one piece of information to hold on to is that most grades are not the same as those that appear on report cards. They are not indications of excellence but refer to the size and shape of the leaf. These are important because they affect the color of the tea and the speed at which it infuses. And they are a factor used in creating blends. Black, green, and oolong teas have different groupings—just to keep things interesting. Familiarity with these grades is simply one more tool that can be used in choosing a tea. It helps to have a map when you're exploring, as these categories are only main roads. Once you know the territory, the best guide is your own taste.

BLACK TEA

The main distinction in grades is between *leaf* grades and *broken* grades. The most familiar and wrongly used words in the tea lexicon appear here: *orange pekoe*. Unfortunately, because of the way some teas are labeled for sale, orange pekoe seems to be a tea of a certain taste. It is not. Pekoe (pronounced *pek-oh,* not *peek-oh*) is a mispronunciation, to begin with, of a Chinese word meaning *white hairs,* which refers to the downy tips of young tea buds. *Orange* is a mystery that certainly has nothing to do with citrus fruit, but may have something to do with a once-upon-a-time scenting of tea with orange blossoms, or the House of Orange, a reference to royalty that Dutch traders may have used to glamorize tea. Regardless, it has nothing to do with the taste or quality of the tea, only the size of the leaves.

TEA GRADES

For grading purposes, teas are separated into whole leaf and broken leaf. The following categories apply to the teas of India and Sri Lanka (Ceylon):

Whole Leaf

Whole leaf teas give out their color and flavor in brewing more slowly than broken grades.

Orange Pekoe (OP). The largest leaf grade of tea. The leaves are long and wiry and produce a liquor of pale or light color.

Pekoe. Shorter leaves, which make a tea of darker color than orange pekoe.

Souchong. A large, round leaf that steeps to a pale liquor.

Broken Leaf

Broken leaf teas account for approximately 80 percent of the total harvest. They make a quicker-brewing, stronger, darker tea.

Broken Orange Pekoe (BOP). These torn leaves are much smaller than any of the whole leaf grades. The liquors have good color and strength and are the cornerstone of many blends.

Broken Pekoe. Leaves are a bit larger than broken orange pekoe and there is less color to the liquors. Often used as filler in a blend.

Broken Pekoe Souchong. Slightly larger leaves than broken pekoe, and therefore lighter in liquor. Also used as filler.

Broken Orange Pekoe Fannings (BOPF). Much smaller leaves than broken orange pekoe. Consequently, the leaves are quick brewing and have good color.

Fines or Dust. The smallest grade. These make a very quick-brewing, strong tea. They are only used in blends of uniform size, generally in tea bags.

F, T, and *G*. Depending on the country of origin, there are teas that carry the designation *flowery* or *tippy* or *golden* along with orange pekoe such as **Flowery Orange Pekoe (FOP)** or **Tippy Flowery Orange Pekoe (FTOP)** or even **Tippy Golden Flowery Orange Pekoe (TGFOP)**. These teas contain the white tip of the flower bud or the silvery tips of dried tea leaves or the golden color of fired tips, all of which should contribute flavor and fragrance to a cup of tea. Occasionally, an *F* for *Fancy* will precede the other initials *(FTGFOP)*, an indication of a still finer tea.

GREEN TEA

Black tea is far and away the most popular in the West, but green tea is gaining adherents. China is the largest producer, with Japan and Taiwan following. Unlike black, green tea *is* categorized by quality, so the following names should tell you something about the excellence of the tea in your cup. The tea is judged according to the age of the leaf and the way it has been rolled and treated.

Chinese Green Tea

Pinhead Gunpowder. This sounds like the name of an explosive idiot, which, of course, it is not. The description hearkens back to the days of the East India Company, when employees first caught sight of the tea, which they mistook for gunpowder. Tender young and medium-aged leaves, rolled into tiny green balls, are used to make gunpowder tea.

Imperial. In the manufacturing of gunpowder, loosely balled older leaf is sifted out. These leaves become imperial.

Young Hyson. Fine quality leaf rolled long and thin.

Hyson. Named after an East India businessman who imported this tea, Hyson is old leaf rolled in such a way that it looks like a combination of loosely rolled imperial and the long, thin, rolled Young Hyson.

Twankay, Hyson Skin, and *Dust.* These are at the bottom of the Chinese green leaf barrel.

Japanese Green Tea

The Japanese consume so much tea that they barely have any to export. The United States imports most of what the country can spare, but the finest teas are held for the natives and very little of it at that.

Gyokuro. Any tea called *Pearl Dew* must have the delicacy of a morning mist, and that's gyokuro. Only the tenderest young buds of the first flush of especially grown bushes are used in this tea and then they are hand rolled.

Tencha. Take these fragile buds, dry them naturally, and roll them by hand and you have tencha, the only other high-quality Japanese grade. These are the leaves that have the honor of being ground into the powder for the Japanese tea ceremony.

Bencha. An old leaf tea pruned from the plant at the end of the season.

Sencha. The tea found in most Japanese teapots and exported to the United States, about 75 percent of the crop is sencha. It is considered one grade, but there are variations on the theme, both in the leaves plucked and the way they are manufactured. Steaming, rolling, and firing are steps made in preparing all sencha, but there are differences in the process based on geographical location. Ideally, there is a good marriage between leaf and procedure, but, in the end, the quality of the leaf is what counts.

Oolong Tea

Oolong still has a foothold in the Fukien Province of China, but the rest of the world's supply is grown in Taiwan (Formosa). Fukien oolongs have a greenish yellow liquor infused from a more loosely rolled leaf. When Formosa oolongs meet hot water, they turn more brownish yellow. These teas are graded on quality, period, and their designations speak for themselves beginning with *Finest* and working down through *Choice, Superior,* and *Good* to *Standard.*

Black, Green, and Oolong: Names to Know

BLACK TEAS (FERMENTED)

Assam, the northeast India district that grows more black tea than anywhere else in the world, also produces the strongest. Assams are robust, rich, pungent, and full-bodied, with a malty taste and dark amber color.

Ceylon teas, grown in Sri Lanka, vary in quality according to the altitude at which they are grown, the higher the better. Flavor is their forte, and they are used in blends for that purpose. The color of these teas is bright and the aroma pleasant. Ceylon is the place where Thomas Lipton first cultivated tea and began the use of *orange pekoe* as a term for denoting the size of the tea leaf, a designation that is not related to quality. However, the name has become so associated with Ceylon teas that they are often marketed as orange pekoe, implying superiority. Dimbula, Nuwara Eliyha, and Uva are a few excellent districts for these teas.

Darjeeling, a northwest Indian town at close to 7,000 feet, is a place blessed with the conditions to produce a truly superior tea. Finding the best is, of course, the usual challenge. Its flavor has been described as "muscatel" after the rich, sweet wine, and it ranges from full-bodied to delicate. Nilgri, in the Blue Mountains of southern India, is a tea with an earthy fragrance and soft taste similar to Ceylon teas.

Chai is the ubiquitous black tea drink of India, boiled with cinnamon, cardamom, pepper, cloves, and ginger, sweetened with honey and vanilla, and mixed with milk—not exactly a purist's delicate brew, but delicious in its own way. The ingredients to create this whole wondrous potion are now available as a package. It can also be bought as an already packaged drink.

Keemun is the supreme Chinese black tea, but it is still not good enough for the Chinese, who drink primarily green tea. Chinese black tea is called *congou* on the world market, a word stemming from the Chinese word *gongfu* (kung fu), which was associated with the tea in the early nineteenth century. To add to the confusion, the Chinese call all black teas *hongcha,* which means *red tea.* Keemun has a strength comparable to India black teas but with a subtle, slightly sweet flavor with little astringency and a superb bouquet.

Yunnan is a Chinese territory north of Assam, in India. These teas are slightly smoky, full-bodied, rich, and peppery in flavor.

Pu-Er is a Chinese tea that undergoes a second fermenting process and as a result has a unique mustiness. It is not commonly found outside China. However, claims of health benefits from reducing cholesterol and aiding digestion are being made about this tea that will undoubtedly increase the demand.

OOLONG TEAS (PARTIALLY FERMENTED)

Formosa oolong is the product of Taiwan's amazing, small, patch gardens located at sea level, rather than in the mountains. The combination of this particular soil and climate produces the most outstanding oolongs in the world. Fermented more than the mainland oolongs, the very best Formosa oolongs are extremely delicate, but still rich and especially fruity tasting. They are graded in six levels of quality from Fancy and Fanciest on down and are known for their "peachy" flavor. The names of some Formosa oolongs are **Tung-Ting, Shui-Hsien (Iris)**, and **Kang-Kou, (Harbour Tea)**.

Ti Kuan Yin or *iron goddess of mercy* is a mainland China oolong that is very lightly fermented and referred to as "bohea" in English. One of the lovely aspects of Chinese teas is their names, and this one implies the promise of a legend and, of course, there is one involving Kuan Yin, the Goddess of Mercy, an iron statue and a remarkable tea plant. This oolong,

very close to green tea, has a delicate bouquet, intense flavor, fruity taste, and light color. Other Chinese oolongs are named **Shui-Xian (Water Fairy)**, **Ti-Lo-Han**, and **Boa Zhong**.

GREEN TEAS (UNFERMENTED)

The Chinese say "ten thousand teas" for anything that is more than one can count, and that is surely the amount of green teas in China. Some are named for the province they are grown in, so there are many teas such as Hunan green tea. The types of Chinese green tea, as discussed in the first section of this book, are generally Gunpowder, Imperial, Young Hyson, and Hyson. The following list is of tea names.

Dragon's Well (Lung Ching). One of the most famous Chinese green teas, it is produced in Chekiang Province near West Lake in Hangchow. That fact is worth mentioning because the water of this vicinity is said to make a magnificent jade-green Dragon's Well brew. The tea is known for its wonderful green color, aroma, and superb grassy taste. The name, true to Chinese form, is related to the legend of a dragon who creates a well to save the people from a drought. Lion's peak *(shih-feng)* is a tea very similar to dragon's well.

Eyebrow Teas. Chun-Mee, "Precious Eyebrow," is one of the teas that is commonly found in China and exported in great quantities. The name refers to the curved shape of the leaf. Most are of the Hyson and Young Hyson type.

Cloud Teas. Jeweled Cloud *(Bai-Yun)* and White Cloud *(Bao-Yun)* are examples of the *yun wu* or *Cloud* teas, so called for the misty mountains in which they grow. The cloud cover and lack of sun in addition to processing adapted to those conditions produces an unusual-tasting and hard-to-find tea.

Chinese green teas have lovely and alluring names like *After the Snow Sprouting* that suggest the tender shoots of the tea bush and the delicacy of their flavors. Ultimately, the only way to learn about them is to brew them. Try making green tea in a glass for the pleasure of watching the leaves "dance" while imparting their essence to the water. Inhale their discreet aromas, and be patient in developing an appreciation for their authentic, earthy taste.

The Japanese drink green tea exclusively, close to 200 million pounds a year. Very little of the best is exported, however, so superior tea from Japan is difficult to come by. Acquaintance with Japanese teas is covered in these basics:

Gyokuro, *Pearl Dew,* is the country's finest green tea, extraordinary because of the way it is grown, shaded from the sun while the new shoots blossom. Slightly sweet, with a vegetative cast, and mild, this tea is full-bodied with a memorable aroma.

Sencha is the better tea that quenches the thirst of most Japanese. Soothing and fragrant, it is the tea preferred for serving to guests and to drink when eating sushi.

Spiderleg is a type of sencha with a unique, mild flavor. Someone who liked spiders must have given this tea of long, twisted leaves its name.

Bencha is the bottom of the barrel of Japanese green tea made from both old and new leaf.

WHITE TEA

Extremely rare and only Chinese, these are teas unlike any other. And no wonder. Hovered over and plucked at the moment of maturity, the buds of this tea are only steamed, not rolled or fired. There are three names to be aware of: *Yin Chen* (Silver Needles), *Pai Mu Tan* (White Peony), and *Ying Mei* (Noble Beauty). Pluck them from the shelves if you find them.

Who Was Earl Grey Anyway: Tea Blends

"Polly, put the kettle on, we'll all have tea."

—CHARLES DICKENS (1812–1870)
BARNABY RUDGE

An orchestra is a synthesis of instruments, a football team is an amalgam of players, a crème brûlée is a marriage of eggs and cream, and most teas we drink are blends. Greatness in tea, like many arts, is almost always a group effort. The few teas that can stand alone are called *self-drinkers,* and they are few indeed. Tea companies create blends that their customers can count on. But not all blends are created equal. So, if you like a blend like English Breakfast, explore the differences in brands. You may be surprised at what you find.

English Breakfast is everywhere—and nowhere is there a common recipe. Its popularity is based on its dependability. Try an English Breakfast tea and you will get a black tea that is somehow familiar and comforting, not exotic, not challenging to the taste buds, and not a surprise. Which is just what most people want first thing in the morning, a wake-up call that is not going to jolt them out of their routine. Invented over a hundred years ago in Scotland by an Edinburgh tea merchant who simply called it "Breakfast," the tea has been popular ever since. Keemun, the famous China black, is said to be the original base and is still used by some tea merchants. Nearly every tea brand has an English Breakfast, and each blend is different. However, the tenor of the teas are similar:

fragrant and mellow, with a flavor that is complemented by milk. English Breakfast's easy nature is welcoming to beginning tea drinkers: not outstanding but not startling, either.

Irish Breakfast is not for people who like their tea weak and their mornings bland. The Irish are said to like their tea ''strong enough for a mouse to walk on,'' which can only be an understatement for a tea with a very hearty body. Assam based, for the most part, Irish Breakfast is a medium strong, black tea blend that really is favored by the Irish, a people who are serious about their tea. Milk is a good counterpoint to this tea's strength.

Russian Caravan is not what it used to be. No one knows what it used to be since the last time a camel carried tea across the continent to Russia from China was the turn of the twentieth century. The current blends have more in common with each other than the original. All its components are black teas with at least some Lapsang Souchong, the element that imparts an undercurrent of smokiness. A strong, dark tea with a characteristic aroma, it is generally served with milk and sugar.

House blends are the rather pedestrian label for the superb tea combinations put together by some of the finest tea merchants in the world. Many are exclusive to a single company and some have historical contexts, like J. P. Morgan Tea, the personal blend of the famous mogul who, it turns out, was a tea lover. A tea that combines Formosa oolongs with black teas, it is available from Simpson & Vail in New York, whose originator formulated the tea for Mr. Morgan. Another example is a blend called Palm Court, centerpiece of the elegant afternoon tea at New York's Plaza Hotel, served in the grand room of that name. Harney & Sons, a Connecticut company, created this sumptuous tea to match the surroundings. In the tea world, these are equivalent to a famous chef's exclusive recipe, and they are only two of many fine connoisseur teas worth investigating. Any opportunity to sample a fine tea company's proprietary brand label, as it is called, is a good one. Most can be purchased at specialty stores or by catalogue.

The *Earl* in *Earl Grey* is a title, not a name. Mr. Charles Grey (1764–1845) was a nobleman and one of the early

English enthusiasts of tea. In his day, tea merchants would put together personal blends for customers, and the earl had his own recipe, rumored to be given to him by a Chinese Mandarin. Historical context does not exactly support this theory, but tea romantics do enjoy it. Earl Grey is the first scented tea the West ever put its nose to, and the fragrance is oil of bergamot, a Mediterranean citrus fruit. Cultivated for the perfume industry and this particular tea, oil of bergamot gives Earl Grey its distinctive taste and aroma. Like English Breakfast, there's an Earl Grey in every tea merchant's lineup, and no two are exactly alike. Mild, smoky, aromatic, with a hint of sweetness, Earl Grey, a blend of India and Ceylon black teas, is the second most popular tea in the world. Earl Grey, really a scented tea, is categorized here under blends because it is one of the world's most well-known.

Sweet, Savory, and Smoky: Scented, Spiced, and Flavored Teas

Teas,
Where small talk dies in agonies.

—PERCY BYSSHE SHELLEY
(1792–1822)

Jasmine is not just for flower lovers. The most popular flower-scented tea, Jasmine is a delightful Chinese creation made with green or pouchong (slightly fermented) teas and the blossoms of the jasmine bush, a combination that can be either sublime or terrible, depending on the quality of the tea and personal taste. The Chinese, who have been perfecting the manufacturing technique since Jasmine became the rage in the third century, designate quality gradings for the tea, so there are definite differences to be aware of. Extra Fancy is, of course, better than Standard. One of the best is Yin Hao, (Silver Down) and other fine examples are Chung Feng (Spring Wind) and Chung Hao (Spring Down). Although you may enjoy the idea of flowers in the tea, whether they appear or not will not affect the taste.

Other scented teas include *chamomile,* which has a light, bittersweet, apple flavor; expensive *chrysanthemum;* delicate flavored *clover;* lemony *hibiscus;* and sweet, aromatic *lavender.* Teas are also scented with orange blossoms, which makes a fragrant, refreshing tea, and even roses, which impart

a delicate, exotic flavor. All these and others are a literal tea party in the garden. If these teas remind you of Victorian women who swooned with the "vapors," they are probably not for you. However, *mint* tea falls into this category, and mint tea over ice is something that many people, especially in the American South, could not live without.

Lapsang Souchong is the Cuban cigar of teas, and like cigars, you may find it repulsive or divine. Produced only in China's Fujian province and Taiwan, the tea is wood smoked, but not in the same way that chicken is grilled over mesquite. When the process is complete, the tea is impregnated with pine smoke. When it's brought back to life in boiling water, there's no mistaking that it's been cured in a smoke-filled room. One telltale whiff is enough. Lapsang Souchong may be the most potent black tea, assertive, smoky, and full-bodied. There are those people who love it and those who definitely do not.

Spiced teas are probably the equivalent of Hawaiian Punch to tea connoisseurs, but that is not to say they can't be delicious, especially on days when the only thing that will unlock your psyche from the winter blahs is something hot and sweet. Herbs and spices like ginger, nutmeg, and cloves are some of the usual suspects in spiced teas, any of which are a matter of personal taste. Some names offer no clues to what's actually going on in the tea, so it's best to read the labels. Constant Comment is *the* case in point. Ruth Campbell Bigelow whipped up the recipe for this spiced tea on her kitchen stove, introduced it to the world in the 1940s, and built a tea empire on its taste. Others, and some are very good, like Nutmeg & Cinnamon and Lemon Tea speak up for what they are.

Flavored teas are a more contemporary category of teas

enhanced by or, some might say, adulterated by fruit flavoring. These are not herbal teas, which are another matter, but black tea with the addition of fruit. The possibilities are infinite and wonderful or deplorable, depending on your point of view. From passion fruit and mango to apricots and kiwi, everything in God's bountiful basket seems to be making its way into tea. If you have a taste for such tea, there are blends with a balance and subtlety that make them very appealing. And good black tea combined with quality dried fruit can make one fine iced tea.

Learning the Lingo: Tea Talk

Tea, though ridiculed by those who are naturally coarse in their nervous sensibilities . . . will always be the favored beverage of the intellectual.

—THOMAS DE QUINCEY (1785–1859)

Like any enterprise, tea tasting has its buzzwords, but neither jargon nor an articulate vocabulary can truly express the qualities of tea. Its essence is ineffable. Like so much that only the senses can communicate, words are poor conveyers of the experience. Nonetheless, the following are phrases used in tea parlance. Words are all we have.

LEAF CONDITION
Criteria
Purity: Free from stalks, twigs, dust, or fibers.

Well-dried: The quality of the drying or firing.

Descriptions
Bloom: A gloss on black leaf that has not been handled a great deal.

Bold: Oversized leaf for the grade of tea.

Clean: Free from stalks, twigs, dust, or fibers.

Burnt: Very overfired; *dry* is overfired, but not burnt.

Even: Consistency in the size of the leaf.

Uneven: Not of consistent size, probably because of poor sorting.

Leafy: Particularly large or long leaf size.

Flaky: Leaf that is flat without a good curl.

Mushy: Leaves that are too moist.

Ragged: Tea that has been manufactured poorly.

Tippy or *Gold Tip*: Tea with young leaf and buds. The tips become gold as they are stained by tea oils in manufacturing.

Well-Twisted: Whole leaf tea that is well-withered and tightly rolled.

COLOR
Criteria

All the following terms refer to the *liquor,* the tea you see in your cup. *Brightness* and *clarity* are the two words used to describe a tea that has a lively translucence; a clearness and freshness to its liquor.

Descriptions

Bright: A color said to be *sparkling,* a term used for all fine teas. *Bright* can also refer to the taste.

Dull: Opaque, the opposite of bright. Also called *muddy.*

Colory: A liquor that has depth.

Green: Refers to the liquor of inferior black tea. May be caused by immature leaves or poor rolling. Not related to teas of a greenish tint or real green tea.

Light: A tea without much color; also refers to its lack of body.

Copper, Orange, Amber: Good colors to see in your tea.

Heavy: Strong-colored liquor, usually lacks liveliness.

TASTE

Criteria

Stepping into this truly subjective area armed with only words is a bit arrogant, but tea tasters must be able to define what their palates are telling them. *Flavor* is the ultimate quality, but it remains elusive in both the teas themselves and the language to describe it. True flavor is most often found in slow-growing teas at higher altitudes.

Pungency: A kind of astringency. A pungent tea is said to have the three B's: *bite, briskness,* and *brightness.*

Point: A tea is said to have point or be pointy if it has some outstanding characteristics.

Body: This term is for a mouth feel. A tea taster's tongue can tell the weight of a tea's liquor, which might be full or light, words that can be applied to almost any drinkable liquid. The tongue can define it best without words.

Mellowness: No tea, no matter what its flavor, should be coarse or harsh. Even strong tea can be mellow.

Descriptions

Delicate, bitter, mild, subtle, flat, sturdy, metallic, harsh, robust—speak the self-explanatory language of the tea taster.

Bite: A term for black tea that refers to its pucker-up astringency.

Brassy: A tangy, metallic undertone.

Brisk: Overused by advertising, but the right term for the lively, refreshing taste of good tea.

Complex: Characteristic of fine teas in which good qualities blend to create a drink more than the sum of its parts.

Fruity: A pleasant tartness found in oolongs and some Keemuns.

Malty: A word that comes from the taste of grains, but far more subtle than that. Found in Assams.

Muscat or *Muscatel*: Reminiscent of the muscat grape, often particular to Darjeelings.

Piquant: Pleasantly pungent or tart.

Plain: A barely adequate tea with nothing really wrong, but nothing noteworthy.

Pungent: A pleasant sharpness or bite. A lively tea will have pungency. Similar to astringent, also a good quality in the right balance.

Strong: Brisk, full, and pungent, without bitterness.

Thick: A positive term that refers to a richness in color and taste. The opposite is *thin*, a tea without much color or taste.

Stewed or *Stewy*: As unattractive as it sounds. A tea that lacks point, and is bitter, perhaps from brewing too long.

Weedy: An interesting quality in green teas—a flavor reminiscent of vegetation. Also *woody*.

AROMA
Criteria

Part of the pleasure of some teas is the fragrance that rises in the steam as the leaves infuse. The aroma, which comes from the leaf and the liquor, may range from spicy to sweet, delicate to intense, but it should be distinct and pleasing.

Description

Nose: Another word for the fragrance or aroma.

Bouquet: Another word for the whole olfactory experience.

Flowery: In the search for the right word, a comparison to flowers to describe a tea's aroma.

Tarry: Smokiness, a scent found with teas like Lapsang souchong that are smoked over wood or charcoal.

UNDESIRABLES
Criteria

Some teas have especially unsavory characteristics as a result of inadequate growth, manufacturing, or storage. They are simply unacceptable. Tea has so much good to offer, one should never tolerate the bad.

Descriptions

Burnt: Speaks for itself and as unappealing as burnt toast. *Bakey* is similar, but not as intense.

Coarse: Harsh on the tongue and unpleasant all around; also called *rasping*.

Gone Off: Way off—stale and no longer palatable; may be tainted or moldy.

Sweetish: Another word for tea that has gone off.

Musty: Tastes the way your basement may smell.

Sweaty: Worse—tastes the way sweat smells. May be a bacterial infection in the tea.

Choosing a Tea
to Love

An Open Mind and an Adventurous Spirit

If you are cold, tea will warm you.
If you are too heated, it will cool you.
If you are depressed, it will cheer you.
If you are excited, it will calm you.

—WILLIAM GLADSTONE (1809–1898)

It may be said that tea is an acquired taste, but that would be wrong. What you acquire, as you become acquainted with tea, is an ability to discern the differences, the tastes and complexities, the flavors and aromas of tea. Contrary to the language of tea, which can be a bit highfalutin, tea is down to earth. To learn about tea, all you need is the equipment you were born with: a set of taste buds and a desire to please your palate. You must bring your awareness to the taste, the fragrance, and the way a tea feels in your mouth. If you pay attention, the knowledge will come easily, one sip at a time.

Putting tea on paper is a little like describing snowflakes. They're both multidimensional and almost impossible to nail down with words. As no two snowflakes are the same, a single-named tea, like Assam, designated by geographical location, is actually many teas that can never be the same. Even a tea from the same garden cannot be identical from one year to the next.

That is all the more reason to rely on your personal preferences. You don't have to be an expert, but you do have to obliterate every mouthful of ordinary tea-bag tea from your memory and start with a *tabula rasa* for tea, ''a mind before it receives the impressions gained by experience.'' Because coming to tea with an open mind is an entirely new experience. The following are some hints about teas you may try. The real impressions will be your own.

TEA ON THE LOOSE

Loose leaves have a lot to tell you—about tea, not fortunes— so take them right in hand and get acquainted. Give them a squeeze test and see if they feel hard but not brittle and have some resiliency to the touch. They shouldn't be so dry as to crumble. Leaves of a good black tea are—and this is a broad generality with many exceptions—small, uniform, and hard to the touch. They may or may not be tippy, that is show buds or very young leaves that have turned white or golden in the manufacturing process. Tips should be well-twisted and long. Tippiness is not necessarily an indication of better tea, because there are other factors, but for the most part, good tip shows that the owner thought well enough of the leaf to manufacture it carefully.

Oolong tea leaves are different, not only in color but also in size and shape. Fine oolongs have open leaves that are curled at the edges rather than twisted, and they have white tip. They are souchong, large flat leaves, somewhere in between green and brown with a reddish hue.

The leaves of green tea are, well, green, a deep olive shade, closest to tea's original on-the-bush color. The most famous Chinese is Gunpowder, which is grayish green and rolled into a tightly compact pellet, from which the tea gets its name. But Chinese Young Hysons have long, twisted leaves and Dragon Well teas look flat and smooth. Japanese Gykuro has leaves that are short and pointy and resemble pine needles, a reason some are called spiderleg. Some Japanese Senchas have a sheen that makes them look polished.

The most striking note about observing leaves is their amazing variety, and that may be the best introduction to tea of all. For once tea has caught your eye, literally, you begin to realize its enormous possibilities. But what is truly magical is to watch "the agony of the leaves," as they unfold in the water, releasing everything that has been imparted to them from rainfall and sun to fermenting, withering, rolling, and firing. When their goodness has become a fragrant drink, the spent leaves are, again, wonderful to examine. So different from when they began, so changed in size, color, and texture, they are visible testimony to the transformation from plant to tea.

A TEA OF YOUR OWN

Transforming yourself into a tea drinker is essentially a delightful trial-and-error enterprise, a path that leads you on with ever greater promises, some of which will actually be fulfilled. Few people are passionate about tea at the beginning, for it is the kind of pleasure that insinuates itself into your life slowly and, suddenly, you can't do without it. Considering what you might like from tea during a day is one way of beginning to choose teas. The suggestions here are offered with this approach in mind.

Morning Tea

English Breakfast or Irish Breakfast, of course, or anything with *breakfast* in its name. These are all black tea blends. Irish is stronger, mostly made from Assam teas from India, and English is originally made from Keemun teas from China, but today may also include Ceylon teas from Sri Lanka. Breakfast teas are often taken with milk. What to expect:

Assams are hearty teas, full-bodied, pungent, and distinguished by a malty taste.

Keemuns share the full-bodied quality but are more subtle with less astringency and a slightly sweet overtone.

Ceylon teas are the most flavorful and aromatic of the teas in breakfast blends.

Midmorning Tea

The stride of the morning calls for a tea that will keep pace with the day, not one that will wind you down. For a deeply

satisfying cup, try a Darjeeling, and for a touch of fruit when you could use a little sweetness, a Black Currant tea is lovely. These are black teas. What to expect:

Darjeelings from India have a wide range from delicate to full-bodied, but they are known for muscat flavor reminiscent of the muscatel grape. Darjeelings tend to be astringent, but those from Nilgri are softer teas. Milk is often used with these teas.

Black Currant, when prepared with natural flavor, is not too sweet and still hearty. This is not a frivolous tea, but one that gives you a good, fortifying mouthful.

Mealtime Tea

Lunch or dinner, some people drink tea with their meals. Oolongs are a very good choice for dining, especially at the evening meal, because they are lower in caffeine. Gykuro, the superior green tea from Japan, is an interesting accompaniment because it is mild but still substantial. What to expect:

Oolongs are known for their pale, peachy flavor. Their natural fruitiness is not to be mistaken for teas to which fruit has been added. They are far more delicate and have a wonderful bouquet. Formosa Oolongs are the ones to choose. They are often taken plain without sugar or lemon.

Gykuro, a Japanese green tea, tends to be herbaceous in taste and aroma. The fact that the flavor may be close to lawn clippings may not sound appealing, but it's definitely worth a try.

Afternoon Tea

Afternoon is a time for a lively tea to revive spirits and energy. It should also be substantial enough to keep you going until your evening meal. Earl Grey is a favorite any time of day, but is especially nice for its touch of citrus in the afternoon. For a hearty, distinctive choice, there is Lapsang Souchong, not everybody's cup of tea, but definitely unique. In between these two is a Russian Caravan or Russian Country, blends with just a touch of Lapsang Souchong's flavor. What to expect:

Earl Grey is one of the world's most popular teas because it is so accessible. A blend that is aromatic with a hint of smokiness and a touch of sweetness, Earl Grey is stimulating without being obtrusive.

Lapsang Souchong is the famous smoked tea that has the scent and taste of the pine wood that impregnated it. This tea is a meal in itself for those who enjoy it, and it will sustain you the rest of the afternoon.

Russian Caravan is a black tea blend that includes a small element of Lapsang Souchong. Although the smokiness is just a low note, this is a strong tea usually taken with milk and sugar.

Tea for Dessert

These teas are for any time your sweet tooth is aching. They are not peaches and cream, but their fruitiness is so appealing and satisfying that they are almost chocolate; as a matter of fact, there are even chocolate-flavored teas. Tea purists may wince, but here are a few flavors that are available. The exact combination depends upon the brand: mango, ginger, peach, almond cream, apricot, orange, passion fruit, bourbon, vanilla, and more.

What to expect: Anything. Choose a quality tea to begin with, and the flavoring will be subtle, delicious, and not overpowering. The aroma of these teas is wonderful.

Tea for Fun

Enjoying tea is like the rest of life's pleasures. In order to expand your indulgences, you have to seek out opportunities. So try Jasmine, a scented Chinese green tea, or two Japanese greens, Gen Mai Cha and Hoji Cha. And don't miss Chai, which is the everyday Indian spiced tea. All of them will surprise you, and each will provide an entirely different tea experience. What to expect:

Jasmine is just what it sounds like, a tea scented with jasmine flowers. Usually green or the slightly fermented pouchang, Jasmine is an ethereal tea as light as air and very fragrant with flowers. If you don't like feeling like a bee homing in on a blossom, this tea is not for you, but it's still an education in a classical Chinese tea.

Gen Mai Cha is a Japanese green tea with an unusual addition. It has barley in it, but it's more like popcorn than grain. The barley has been popped and imparts a very interesting flavor.

Hoji Cha is also a Japanese green, and this is a roasted tea. It has a nutty, toasty flavor that is quite different.

Chai is a delicious Indian spiced tea with cloves and cardamom and ginger that is brewed with milk and sugar. There's a recipe in the tea drinks section at the end of this book, or you can buy house blends.

Evening Tea

Tea has often been noted as an instrument of meditation. At the very least, it can be soothing and relaxing. Finding a tea of your own that has this effect is a small search for tranquillity that can have a large impact. Of course, such a tea is salutary at any time, but in the evening, a tea that eases the tensions of the day is especially beneficial. Green tea is the tea of choice in this regard. With the least caffeine and any number of health-giving properties, green tea is more refreshing than it is stimulating and more quieting than energizing. In addition, any number of herb teas are said to be inducements to repose. The most available Chinese green teas are Gunpowder and Dragon's Well or Lung Ching. For a combination of both a green tea and herbal infusion effect, there are some green teas combined with mint. What to expect:

Gunpowders or *Pearl Tea,* as the Chinese call this tea that looks like tight little balls, has a light body and a slightly spicy flavor.

Dragon's Well has a grassier taste with sweet overtones.

Minted Green Tea, which can be found with various titles by different brands is, of course, minty, smooth, and very cleansing.

Tea is so accessible that you don't even have to leave the house to have it. The following companies have catalogues for the asking and sell teas by mail. Most are extremely informative, offer clear descriptions of their teas, and also sell all the accoutrements you need from teapots to cozies. Many encourage expanding your tea horizons by offering small, inexpensive packages for sampling.

The Republic of Tea 1-800-298-4TEA

Harney & Sons 1-800-TEA-TIME

Stash Tea 1-800-826-4218

The Tea Club 1-800-FULL-LEAF

Peet's Coffee & Tea 1-800-999-2132, ext. 220

James Norwood Pratt Luxuries 1-800-JNP-LUXT

Robert & Joseph Ltd. 1-414-566-2520 or 414-566-2275

Silk Road Teas 1-415-488-9015

Upton Tea Imports 1-800-234-TEAS

If you are a person who is confused by too many choices, tea may be a bit overwhelming at first. The Chinese saying,

"Ten thousand teas," when expressing an infinite amount, did not come into being by accident. But tea only has to be taken one tea at a time, and each one is an experience that will excite you to choose another. Almost unconsciously, you will become bolder in your choices and more daring in your tastes. Tea, contrary to its image, is not for the timid, for it inspires an adventurous spirit in the quest for better and better tea. Along the way, you will acquire knowledge, and, yes, taste, for choosing the tea you love.

The Perfect Cup: Making Tea

Boiling, Steeping, and Drinking: The Way to Brew

The hot water is to remain upon it [the tea] no longer than whiles you can say The Misere Psalm very leisurely.

—SIR KENELM DIGBY (1603–1665)

B rewing tea is simplicity itself, and so it may be mistaken for ordinary. But as you become attuned to the nuances of taste and the subtleties of flavor, as you begin to anticipate the goodness of the cup, the everyday tasks involved become pleasurable, even ceremonial. It is a quiet process in which, as your knowledge increases, you gradually and imperceptibly become immersed.

Being new to tea is like approaching any new pastime; for example, when you take up tap dancing, first you learn the steps, and even though you're delighted, no one is going to mistake you for Gene Kelly. So it is with tea. Like dancing, the finesse develops slowly, evolving into grace and even beauty. To begin with, all you need is a teapot, a kettle, cold water, loose tea or tea bags, a willingness to be surprised, and these directions:

Bring the water to a full boil.

Heat the teapot by rinsing it with hot tap water or some of the boiling water.

Place in the pot one teaspoon of loose tea for each six-ounce cup, plus one for the pot. Or use one tea bag for each cup.

Bring the teapot close to the kettle and pour in the boiling water.

Steep for three to five minutes, depending on the type of tea.

Remove the leaves or bag, stir, and pour.

These are the steps to the dance of tea. The following are the refinements that make the difference between just knowing what to do and moving to the music with elegance and style.

WATER WAYS
Water

In the eighth century, Lu Yü, exacting tea drinker that he was, recommended water from mountain streams. He found river water to be second best, and he definitely had reservations about wells. He even preferred slow-flowing streams and stone-lined pools, but that seems a bit fussy. Today, our alternatives are more concerned with the taint of technology than the bubbles in a waterfall. Most tap water, even the best, is chlorinated or fluoridated, and many bottled waters have a high mineral content. Water does effect the taste of tea. The most practical solution is a simple charcoal filter device for the faucet or the type of small jug that can be kept in the refrigerator. Always start with fresh, cold water. Water can kill the taste of tea if its oxygen has been flattened by sitting around or if it has been boiled before.

THE BOILING POINT
Boiling

If you've ever waited for water to boil, you know that there's boiling and then there's *boiling*. In making tea, the water tem-

perature counts. Since brewing with a thermometer in hand
seems just a little excessive, you need to tune in with your
eyes and ears. Water boils at 212° Fahrenheit, and that's the
right heat for most black and oolong teas. When you see a
stream of steam shooting up from the kettle spout, or in Lu
Yü's exotic view, when the water "leaps like breakers ma-
jestic and resounds like a swelling wave," rinse the teapot
with hot water, bring it close to the kettle, and get ready. The
conventional wisdom is that you will lose the boil if you have
to take the time to bring the kettle to the pot.

On the other hand, you can take your time with green tea.
Boiling water is too, too much for its delicate leaves. So don't
bring the water to a full boil. As a matter of fact, it should
never be too hot to touch. Watch for steam just curling out
of the spout for the right temperature, which is about 180°.
Green tea unfolds languorously in this embracing warmth.

One more caution: It's possible to *over*boil water, bubbling
away the oxygen and along with it, the liveliness of the tea.
The water's right when it comes to a boil, a moment you will
easily recognize as you acquire tea sense.

YOUR CUP OF TEA

Tea

Choose the best tea that you can afford, the tea that strikes
your fancy, the tea that you think will energize or soothe you,
warm or cool you. Tea is a matter of taste, and there's nothing
more personal. Choose loose tea or tea in bags, but if you are
interested in tea, loose tea is the way to develop your taste.
Keep it in a tight container in a dry place, safe from exposure
to air and nearby odors. Take a moment to look at the tea
before you brew. Notice the length and size of the leaves, the
color, and the tightness or looseness of the twist. As you
become more familiar with tea types, the dry leaves will teach
you, not about your future, but about what kind of tea you
like.

How much to use is a different matter. The one teaspoon
per cup and one for the pot rule is a general one, probably
invented for the sake of convenience. Weaker or stronger

brews are a relative measure depending on who's doing the drinking. So sip until you know and then choose the amount that seems right for the tea and the drinker.

TEA TIMING

Steeping

Here, again, is where there are rules and there are preferences. The rules are three minutes for green tea and up to five or even seven minutes for black and oolong tea. These are fine parameters to start with, but taste is your only true judge, and experience is your only guide. How long you steep your tea depends on how strong you like it, but there are a few guidelines.

Tea is an infusion. That is, the essential oils of the leaves are released when submerged in water. To achieve an infusion of a certain balance, the water must be the right temperature and the timing *must be right* as well. The leaves must have enough time to open up and release their color, flavor, and aroma. If the timing is too short, the tea will be weak, but if it is too long, the tea will be *stewed*, not brewed, and black tea, especially, will become bitter. You can experiment to discover the perfect timing for a particular tea for you, but you cannot be casual about it. Be exact, even use a timer. A small difference in timing makes a huge difference in taste.

Generally, the larger the leaf, the longer the steeping time. A small leaf has more surface exposed to the water and, therefore, it will infuse more quickly. A larger leaf needs to steep longer. The leaves in bags, which of necessity are small, infuse very quickly and can turn bitter all too soon. Delicate green teas take the minimum time for steeping, and black teas take longer.

COLOR BLIND

Remember, the clock and your taste are your guides, *not* the color. The color is the first element imparted from black tea leaves. If you take out the leaves when the color appears, you will never get to the good part—the flavor and body. With green tea, there is never much color; the pale liquor is its trademark. Wait for more color and you may stew the tea. Keep in mind the old cliché that you can't judge a book by its cover, and never depend on color as an indicator of brewing time. One of the bonuses of tea is the glorious variety of colors, a palette that stimulates your senses and enhances your pleasure.

THE LEAVES LEAVE THE POT
Removing the Leaves

At various times in history and in different societies, brewed tea leaves were eaten. A little butter and salt, and lunch was on the table. Assuming that is not your plan, you must discard the leaves, or at least keep them out of your cup. If you're going to use all the tea brewed at once, the handiest device is a strainer. This little perforated instrument of stainless steel, silver, or ceramic fits neatly over the cup as you pour, catching any leaves swimming up the spout of the pot. Another sensible alternative is to use two pots. Keep a second handy, warmed with hot water, and simply transfer the tea, leaving the leaves behind in the original pot. For all other equipment, and there are alternatives, see the next section, which begins on page 94.

Of course, if you are using tea bags, there is no mystery to retrieving them or preparing the tea. Always use freshly boiled water and allow the bag to steep three to five minutes. When removing the bag, let it drip into the cup, but resist squeezing it. The brewed leaves pressed in this way could impart a bitter flavor.

HOW DO YOU TAKE YOUR TEA?

Drinking

What you add to your tea is, in tea parlance, what you *take*. And what you take is sugar, milk, or lemon. Any of the above or none. Notice that cream is missing from the list. Its richness is just too much for the taste of tea.

We tend to think of England as the arbiters of these matters, but the Chinese were putting milk in their tea long before the English, and long before Queen Victoria first experienced lemon in her tea in Russia. Today, what you take in your tea is anything you like. Milk is fine with black teas, and an improvement with some, softening and smoothing the liquor. But milk is never added to green or oolong teas. Once upon a time, etiquette demanded that milk be added first, but it makes far more sense to add it after the tea is poured when the amount can be more easily adjusted. Lemon and milk are mutually exclusive because lemon will curdle milk. Milk is best served at room temperature so that it will not cool the tea excessively. Sugar is a matter of taste and is rivaled by honey as a delicious sweetener. And lemon is, well, astringent, just one more way in which tea can be prepared, as it should be, to please the drinker.

Whatever method you choose, bring attention to your tea. Fill your mouth to feel its body. Inhale the aroma. Drink tea with full awareness, and it will teach you what you need to know.

MULTI-BREW

Brewing Tea for a Crowd

Tea is certainly one drink you can drink alone, but sharing tea with friends is an experience with its own delights. If you have a *lot* of friends, serve them tea made from a concentrate, then add boiling water to each cup. First, boil about a quart of water. Pour that over about two-thirds of a cup of tea leaves, stir, and steep for five minutes or longer, but not much longer. Strain the liquor into another pot. At this point the liquor can stand for a few hours. When serving, add a teaspoon or two of the concentrate to each cup, depending on the strength desired, and fill with freshly boiled water. At two teaspoons per cup, the concentrate will make about twenty-four cups.

ON ICE
Iced Tea

To some people, tea was ordained to be iced. Not true. But if it's summer and it's hot, nearly everyone is glad that iced tea was invented. To make enough iced tea for a group, follow the same measurements as for hot tea for a group: two-thirds of a cup of tea leaves to one quart of water. Steep for five minutes, then strain this concentrate into a container with three quarts of cold water. The total will be about a gallon of iced tea. Pour into tall glasses over ice. Serve with sugar and lemon and a sprig of mint for a garnish.

To use tea bags, experiment with the strength that suits you. Eight to ten tea bags per quart of water are recommended. For one quart, simply boil the water, steep the bags, remove them, and pour the tea over ice into the glasses. If you want to make more than a quart, boil one quart and make a concentrate with the number of tea bags necessary for the greater volume. Remove the bags and pour the concentrate into a container with the additional cold water.

Teapots to Tea Bowls: Tools for Tea

We had a kettle; we let it leak:
Our repairing made it worse;
We haven't had any tea for a week . . .
The bottom is out of the Universe

—RUDYARD KIPLING (1865–1936)

Nothing is less daunting than the basic equipment you need to brew tea. You can brew tea by placing a teaspoon of tea or a tea bag in your cup—end of story. But there are variations on the theme. Some are designed to make it easier to combine and then separate the leaves from the tea. Any can become part of your own personal tea ceremony.

SHORT AND STOUT

The Teapot

The section starting on page 101 describes teapots as an art form, but this discussion is strictly utilitarian. A teapot has to *work*, so its design must include a functional form. And it should work *for you*, so be a discerning shopper and aim for perfection. Grip the handle to make sure that it fits your fist and that your knuckles don't press against the pot—a bad idea when it's hot. Check the lid to see that it has a knob and that the edge is deep enough to anchor it when you pour. Examine the spout. Its base should be higher than the level at which the leaves would collect, and its top should be as high as the pot. Some pots have built-in infusers (see below) to remove the leaves, an advantage if you are fastidious by nature. Never buy a metal pot (think of the taste of *that* in your tea). If you choose ceramic, you'll be stepping into a long tradition, but if you are enchanted by the dance of the tea leaves as they unfold in boiling water, pick glass. You won't be disappointed. Of course, unlike spouses, you can always have more than one teapot at the same time.

LEAF LOCKERS

The Tea Ball

As if this name were not indelicate enough, these devices have also been called tea eggs. Only the stainless steel wire mesh type are recommended, not the aluminum perforated variety of the eponymous egg shape. These spheres of mesh hold the leaves in a cup or pot, circumventing the mess of loose leaves. There are smaller versions, made especially for one cup, that look like a giant safety pin with a ball on the end. The larger size, for the pot, has a chain and hook on the end for easy retrieval. The objection to these is that the leaves are cramped and lack the room to expand and infuse with full flavor. To be sure, you should never fill them completely, for that would really compress the leaves. If a pot needs more tea than one can hold with room to grow, use two tea balls. Just think two for tea instead of tea for two.

The Basket Infuser

Infusers are essentially tea balls in another shape—the basket. There are thoroughly modern plastic infusers available in two sizes, and these work very well when you want a little distance from the natural messiness of tea leaves. There are also nylon mesh basket infusers that are built right into teapots and even mugs. They have a handy little grip extender for lifting, and the mug has a lid for holding in the heat. The one element you do give up with these devices is aesthetics. Tea brings us closer to nature, while plastic does not. However, there are ceramic teapots with built-in ceramic infusers, and these are more elegant, and very good, choices.

The Strainer

Here is the little device that allows you to pour tea directly into a cup without interfering leaves. Shaped like a tiny shallow bowl, it fits over the cup, has one handle or two, and sits tidily on an accompanying dish. Although not their intention, strainers are often used as a place to put a used tea bags. Still not a pretty sight, at least the bag has a place to drip. Strainers are a utilitarian shape hard to change, but are available plain and fancy.

The Tea Press Pot

The glass press pot is a simple concept combining a plunger with a strainer on the bottom. Instead of confining the leaves in an infuser, this pot allows the leaves to swim and then separates them from the liquor when they are plunged to the bottom with the strainer. This method does work and offers, for your entertainment, the advantage of a clear view of the leaves. The possible disadvantage is a bitter taste from compressing the leaves after they have infused.

The Tea Caddy

Today, anything that will hold tea airtight and keep it fresh is an acceptable container, but tea *caddy* is the original name. Call your plastic container a caddy or look for something lovelier, but search for a seal that keeps the air out. Many fine teas are sold in tins.

The Cozy

The idea of a padded cloth tea cozy may seem too, too cute, but in fact, these little overcoats for the teapot are very functional. Some are made to pop over the pot like a shawl to shield it from cool breezes. Others are constructed so that the pot can actually wear the cozy, sort of like baby pajamas with feet. The handle, spout, and lid emerge from this cocoon for functional brewing and pouring. The intention, of course, is to keep the tea as hot as possible while the leaves infuse and afterward, a very worthwhile goal. Most cozies are made of printed fabrics, flowers or fruit, no doubt a legacy from their English origins.

Special Teapots

The Yixing teapot, thought to be the forerunner of all modern teapots, has up-to-date versions. These can be bought in several styles, all crafted out of the stoneware believed by some to be the best in the world for brewing tea. Japanese cast metal teapots add the inspirational quality of tradition to the drinking of green tea. Enamel lined, these graceful Asian pots have fine heat retaining qualities.

Chinese Tea Bowls

Created without handles in the Chinese manner, these bowls are made for brewing tea right in the cup. Each comes with a cover to keep the tea hot.

Japanese Tea Bowls

These have no handles and no cover and are commonly used to serve tea in all types of Asian restaurants in the West. Savoring green tea in these little bowls is a lovely way to engage in the spirit of the Japanese tea ceremony.

The Art and
Science of Tea

Objects of Art: The Teapot

There is a great deal of poetry and fine sentiment in a chest of tea.

—RALPH WALDO EMERSON (1803–1882)

Nursery rhymes do simplify: *"I'm a little teapot short and stout. Here is my handle, here is my spout."* There it is, centuries of historical development, social evolution, and artistic endeavor, summed up for the amusement of children. All the utensils used in serving tea are cultural mirrors of their countries: China, Japan, and that European usurper of tea, England. But the teapot, most of all, is a direct link with the past from the seventh century to the twenty-first. Steep tea in a pot and you are steeped in history. Know that when you are pouring tea, you are part of the continuum of civilized humankind. Holding that handle is your link.

MING, YIXING

The handle actually appeared in China during the Ming Dynasty (c. A.D. 1300–1600). Until that time, bowls, in which the tea was both prepared and served, were the most important items in teaware. But in the beginning of the sixteenth century, the discovery of a truly exceptional clay in the Yixing (pronounced *E-shing*) region of China set in motion the development of the humble—and not-so-humble—teapot, a form artists have embellished for centuries. This clay, with its colors ranging from beige to a deep purple brown, was so perfect for molding and firing, so appealing in texture, that many pots were left unglazed.

Beautiful as these teapots were, their natural darker hues were not accepted as sufficiently elegant for the Chinese imperial court where only glazed porcelain was deemed acceptable. So much the better for us, for Yixing wares became the favorite of tea-drinking scholars and poets whose intellectual interest spurred craftsmen to create teapots of fanciful shapes and fine designs. Thus, the teapot became more than a container for holding tea. It became an expression of artistic development.

THE ENGLISH TAKE TO THE TEAPOT

Exactly what vessel with handle and spout inspired the British to become teapot makers to the world is unclear. Some say that the urn-shaped Chinese wine jar, which was literally packed in tea to prevent breakage on the long sea voyages from the Orient to Europe, was the precursor of the Western teapot. A more romantic notion is that Yixing teapots were the first teapots to be imported by the West, bringing with them two dominant styles that have been the basis for creative design ever since. One is the clean line of the classical and the other is the ingenuity of the naturalistic, which turned teapots into everything from pomegranates to monkeys. By the middle of the eighteenth century, British pottery makers, inspired by these designs, began to mass produce teapots to meet the growing thirst of the English for tea.

Josiah Wedgwood and Josiah Spode, whose names are now synonymous with fine china, were among them. Indeed, *china* was what the British called the porcelain imported from that country, and it wasn't until the beginning of the eighteenth century that the product was developed in Europe. The necessary clay was first discovered in Meissen, Germany, and china was first produced there and in Sèvres, France, but by the middle of the century, the tea-drinking British were in the vanguard of teapot and porcelain production. Wedgwood, being the good capitalist that he was, produced elegant teapots for the upper classes and mass-produced pots that were everyman's cup of tea.

TEAPOTS OF THE TIMES

From the middle of the eighteenth century until today, ceramic teapots have been created to match the artistic trends of their times and very often they marched with the avant garde. The middle of the eighteenth century saw teapots in the shapes of cauliflowers and camels as well as pots with elaborately painted scenes and gilt edges. During the nineteenth century, fashion turned to the classical periods of the Renaissance, the Greeks, the Gothic, the Chinese, and the Japanese. To match this trend, teapots were produced that would feel at home surrounded by furniture in any of these styles. The turn-of-the-century Art Nouveau period produced teapots as beautiful and grandiose as the elaborate florals, plants, and birds they imitated.

With the modern art movements in the twentieth century, potters claimed their rightful place as artists of equal stature to painters and sculptors, architects and furniture designers, and created teapots of great wit and imagination. Two opposing trends and the dynamic tension between them transcended chronological art movements and continue today: those who believed that design is predicated on function and those who chose the teapot as simply an object for artistic expression.

In the beginning of the century, teapots were pared down, sleek, modern, and functional. But drinking tea in the 1930s, when Art Deco reigned, meant pouring from pots in the shapes of race cars, airplanes, and even tanks, whose creators regarded machines as art objects. The second half of the century saw teapots as classically functional, whimsical, decorative, and even political. They range in shape from teapots as vampires and werewolves, sinks and plumbing fixtures, to pots of Queen Elizabeth and a chicken-bodied Colonel Sanders. Others, that serve up messages with their tea, take the forms of the towers of a nuclear plant, the bones of a skull, and a hostage teapot draped in chains. All are works of art.

TIMELESS TEAPOTS

As an object of artistic exploration, the humble teapot engaged some of the great talents of the twentieth century, Salvador Dali, Frank Lloyd Wright, and Roy Lichtenstein among them. Indeed, Garth Clark, in his book *The Eccentric Teapot*, quotes art historian Herbert Read on the subject of the teapot as one of pottery's most challenging forms: "The balance of the spout and handle of a teapot, with each other and with the body of the pot, is an aesthetic problem to which no artist need be ashamed to devote his attention." The potters in Yixing, who brought their attention to the problem centuries ago, are still at it—and still seeking new markets. You can find them on the Internet describing their ancient wares in the most modern way possible, proof that teapots are timeless.

Flights of Fancy: Tea Legends

The ancient Chinese invested tea with an aura of the mythical, making its qualities seem ethereal, noble, somehow exalted. Perhaps the people of these civilizations were yearning for beauty in their lives, the antidote to hardship that humans have always sought. And they chose tea, not just as a symbol, but as an expression of what was beautiful and soul satisfying. Out of this impulse comes poetry and fanciful stories, legends and lovely names for tea, all conveying messages of relief from suffering, rewards for moral behavior, and a striving for the ideal.

MONKEY TEA

In Chinese legends, exquisite teas often are named for legends of fantastic events that explain their unearthly goodness. In *The Chinese Art of Tea*, John Blofeld tells the story of Monkey Tea *(Hou-Êrh)*. In this tale, monkeys were just one of the creatures living in the remote and wild mountains where the Buddhist monks of the Heavenly Wisdom Monastery tended their fruit trees and tea bushes. One day, a group of chattering monkeys descended on the pear trees and stripped the ripening fruit. The young novice who witnessed the raid was horrified, but the abbot instructed him to think compassionately of the monkeys who, just like man, he said, have a spiritual nature.

That winter, a particularly difficult one, the monkeys again descended from the mountains fiercely menacing the monks for food. Instead of hoarding his provisions, the abbot presented the monkeys bags and bags of food, which the animals seized greedily and fled. In the spring, the monks climbed into the mountains, burdened by the strenuous work of harvesting tea leaves. Suddenly, monkeys crashed out of the heights dragging with them the same bags, filled with young tender tea leaves, plucked from bushes no human could hope to reach. The tea from these leaves, a brew of extraordinary, even celestial, quality, became known as Monkey Tea.

IRON GODDESS OF MERCY

A far lovelier named tea is Iron Goddess of Mercy *(Ti Kuan Yin)* whose legend also rewards good behavior with good fortune. The narrative begins in the Wu-I Mountains where this tea is grown. A man devotedly pays respects to the statue of an iron *(ti)* goddess in a run-down temple, burning incense and doing what he can to maintain the building. The goddess, Kuan Yin, appears to him in a dream, telling him that a treasure that will bear fruit for generations lies in a cave behind the temple. It is his, but he must share it with his neighbors. The gift is a sprig of tea. The rest is predictable as these myths are, but lovely nonetheless. He plants and tends the sprout and it blossoms remarkably quickly. Its delicious tea brews with an intoxicating fragrance. The man distributes cuttings to all the surrounding farmers who, to this day, produce a tea named for the iron statue in the ruined temple.

HEAVENLY TEA

These and other legends raised tea to a mythical dimension, but the Chinese also exalted tea for its effects, extolling the beverage for virtues ranging from simple thirst quenching to deliverance from sins. During China's Age of Poetry, at the time of the T'ang Dynasty, circa A.D. 600 to 900, the poet Lu T'ung was inspired to attribute tea with deliverance from this world into the next. After *seven* cups of tea, he wrote, transported:

The first cup moistens my lips and throat;
The second cup breaks my loneliness;
The third cup searches my barren entrail but to find
     therein some five thousand volumes of odd
     ideographs;
The fourth cup raises a slight perspiration—all the
     wrongs of life pass out through my pores;
At the fifth cup I am purified;
The sixth cup calls me to the realms of the immortals.
The seventh cup—ah, but I could take no more! I only
     feel the breath of the cool wind that rises in my
     sleeves.
Where is Elysium? Let me ride on this sweet breeze
     and waft away thither.

Does this seem like more than you might expect from a cup of tea—the banishment of loneliness, purification, immortality, and a quick ticket to the Elysian Fields, home of eternal happiness? Perhaps. By the eighteenth century, the Chinese were more earthbound in their views, but still waxed poetic about the benefits of tea. The Emperor Ch'ien Lung (1710–1799) wrote: ''You can taste and feel, but not describe, the exquisite state of repose produced by tea, that precious drink, which drives away the five causes of sorrow.''

We can all list the causes of our sorrow, but who among us can so readily name our deliverance? If for centuries a great civilization, rent by the upheavals of history, found solace in a cup of tea, should we not offer ourselves the same relief? Admittedly, that's a bit grandiose, but why not take it as an inspiration. Bring your attention to your tea and somewhere in the back of your mind, remember that it is brought to you with myths of rescue and renewal, visions of beauty, belief in good fortune, and the joy of peace of mind. Start there and see where it takes you.

The Future in Leaves: Tea Tells Fortunes

Matrons who toss the cup and see
The grounds of fate in grounds of tea.

—ALEXANDER POPE (1688–1744)

Separation, divorce? Change in career? A trip? A move? New partner? Old problem? Illness? Recovery? Questions abound. Tea leaves may be the answer. Or they may not.

The ancient art of reading tea leaves is a worldwide phenomenon. Asians have no monopoly, except in Hollywood, where no one drinks tea but wizened old men who, with eyes creased into foreboding slits, extract ominous news from make-believe leaves. This image is on a par with fortune-tellers depicted as gypsy women with wrist-to-elbow bangle bracelets and wild black hair. People with psychic abilities are not defined by nationalities. Humanity is their domain.

To the uninitiated, it's hard to believe that a cup of soggy tea leaves has anything to say. But like any artful science that seeks to decipher life's serpentine road, reading tea leaves has guideposts, formulas, and ceremonies. With centuries of tradition behind them, readers are not just winging it. The shapes and arrangements of the leaves in the cup speak to them in a language that they have been taught to interpret.

STORIES IN SHAPES

To begin with, the shapes of the leaves are both real and symbolic. They may appear in the shape of a crested moon, a bird, a note, or a letter. Such a moon would imply prosperity. Who among us would not want to know that? And a bird is a lucky sign. In motion, the little winged tea leaf means good news. Sitting on its legs, the bird might point to a fortunate journey. This lexicon of shapes is lengthy and fraught with possible interpretations. The "truth," if there is only one, lies in the ability of the reader to weave together a whole cloth from the strands of shapes before him.

TRUTH IN PLACEMENT

The arrangement of leaves also matters. Imagine your cup and the scattered infused leaves lying there waiting for their cryptic message to be unlocked. The position of the cup's handle represents home and your more personal questions or events. Those leaves closest to this hot spot are related to your most private and family matters. Those on the opposite side of the cup deal with happenings away from home and with strangers (tall, dark, and otherwise). On the right side of the handle are formations with reports of occurrences and people marching into your life. On the left side, these are exiting.

The distance of the leaves from top to bottom of the cup weighs in with news as well. The closer the formations are to the top of the rim, the more immediate the prospects. As they dwindle down to the bottom, the time into the future increases. Readings of these positions may be as specific as the beginning, the middle, and the end of a month or year. Top, middle, and bottom of the cup can be emotional clues, too—happy to sad, from rim to bottom. Come to the cup with a confused state, and the reader may not be able to discern any of this, for, in a sense, the leaves are a mirror of the mind. When they reflect murkiness, no distinct images emerge.

CONSIDERING THE ANSWER

Of course, in times of clarity, we might not come to tea leaves for answers, but who among us is ever without questions? To our last breath, we are wondering about *something* (perhaps, at that moment, we are *most* curious about what happens next). But the future is not the only domain of the leaves; they can be consulted to answer a specific question, too. To take a new job or not, to buy a house or not, to marry or not to marry, that could certainly be *the* question—drink up and ask the leaves. To enter into the mystique, you do first drink the tea. You begin with an infusion of leaves in a plain white cup with a handle. Then, keeping your question in mind, you sip the liquid down to about an inch. Finally, taking the handle in your left hand, you swirl the cup to the left three times, turn it over, and place it on the saucer, handle pointing to the reader. The ceremony may include placing your hand over the cup to radiate more of your personal energy. The rest is up to the reader.

The cup drains, the reader picks it up, and an interaction begins that combines wisdom, intuition, imagination, instinct, creativity, all the elements that are indefinable, innately human, and therefore, all the more enigmatic. The message in the leaves is no more clear-cut than life, but the reader brings all these factors to bear as he turns the cup and studies its contents until images and configurations begin to emerge. He examines their patterns and proximity, for symbols in relation to one another can enhance or negate their messages. No leaf is extraneous; every formation counts.

Ultimately, he considers your question and circumstances, and then he offers what you've been waiting for, his *interpretation*. It does not have the hard facts of statistics or the irrefutable beep of a heart monitor or the deadly evidence of a laboratory slide. Reading tea leaves is an art in the realms of the psychic and emotional. And although the reader's words may ring with unsettling, hopeful, joyful, or dreadful truth, you should never bet your life on them.

The Science of Tea: Health Benefits

My experience . . . convince me that tea was better than brandy, and during the last six months in Africa I took no brandy, even when sick, taking tea instead.

—THEODORE ROOSEVELT (1858–1919)

The Chinese belief in the health benefits of tea is ancient and empirical. Only citizens of the modern world, creatures of science, have the arrogance to demand proof. It seems to be coming. Today, scientists interested in tea and health are making claims based on research, studies, and statistics. There is an increasing body of work. So, if you feel that drinking tea is soothing and stimulating, relaxing and invigorating, you are probably right. And if the newest studies are conclusive, that is only the beginning.

CHEMISTRY AND POLYPHENOLS

Tea is made up of three major chemical components, polyphenols, caffeine, and essential oils, the first two of which are most relevant to well-being. Chemistry, which in the end is the root of everything, offers the most compelling explanation.

Polyphenols, erroneously called tannins, give tea its astringency. During black tea's manufacturing process, the leaves are fermented or, more accurately, oxidized, and so are its polyphenols, which change chemically. In green tea, neither

112

the leaves nor the polyphenols are oxidized; and in oolong, the process is somewhere in between. It is polyphenols that are most interesting in relation to health.

Here's why, simplified. There are chemical agents that arise in body processes called free radicals or *oxidants*. These are aggressive molecules that combine and attack a wide variety of other molecules and cause oxidation, or damage, to cell membranes, genetic material, and other components of living tissue. In other words, they cause destructive change. The results of oxidant behavior range from wrinkles in your skin to the mutations that can cause cancer.

The polyphenols in tea are *antioxidants,* molecules that counteract this process. Their chemical structure, which consists of an atom of oxygen linked to an atom of hydrogen, can combat free radicals by combining with them chemically and neutralizing them before they cause damage. There are different types of polyphenols, but they are all white knights on the cellular level. Green tea has the richest source of disease-fighting polyphenols, but black and oolong teas also contain significant levels.

Research is pointing to the following health benefits from the polyphenols in tea:

Heart Disease

Studies support evidence that tea reduces blood cholesterol and thus lowers the risk of heart disease. In a 1993 Dutch study, an increased consumption of tea, onions, and apples, foods containing polyphenols called flavonoids, in over 800 men, was linked to a lower rate of death from coronary disease.

Cancer

Animal research suggests that drinking black and especially green tea may reduce the risk of cancer. The possibility is that the antioxidant activity of tea's polyphenols helps to prevent the cell mutation that takes place in some cancers.

Immune System

White blood cells are the body's front line of defense and indications are that the polyphenols in tea increase these blood cells and thus help to fortify the body against certain infections.

Tooth Decay

Plaque is the bane of a healthy mouth, adhering to teeth and beginning the process of tooth decay. Tea's polyphenol molecules interact with mouth bacteria, disarming it before it becomes plaque. The flouride in tea also strengthens tooth enamel to resist decay.

Digestion

Polyphenols and essential oils work to increase the muscular aspects of digestion and the production of digestive juices. It has also been suggested that polyphenols act as an antibacterial in gastric diseases such as dysentery.

And there's more. Some scientists have suggested that if tea reduces fat in the blood, it might also reduce fat in tissues, which would imply that a tea "diet" would promote weight loss. But the only absolute dietary news in relation to tea is that a cup of the brew has only four calories. It also has some nourishing vitamins. Green tea is a source of vitamin C. And a simple, satisfying, seemingly innocent cup of tea contains vitamin E, carotene, and selenium, all valuable agents in fighting oxidation.

THE CAFFEINE CONNECTION

Most teas also contain caffeine. People crave, abuse, praise, and avoid caffeine. Some can't get through the day without it, others claim they can't live with it. Tea has it, but not as much as coffee. Fermented tea has more than unfermented. The rules of the cup and caffeine are:

Coffee has more than twice as much caffeine as tea. A cup of coffee has about 120 milligrams of caffeine. Black tea has about 50 milligrams, oolong has about 30 milligrams, and green tea has only 20 or less. Tea bags, which are made up of the smallest leaf pieces, deliver more caffeine, all at once, while loose leaf tea releases less more slowly. Obviously, in all cases, these are approximations; the amount of caffeine depends on the strength of the brew.

Caffeine stimulates the nervous system, sending wake-up calls both to the brain and the body, fighting fatigue, increasing alertness, and rousing the heart, lungs, and muscles. In coffee, these messages are rather immediate; with tea, they take up to fifteen minutes. One could, and people do, argue about these effects and their relative benefits or harm, but science has, so far, not provided any definitive answers. Common sense says that tolerance to caffeine is an individual matter.

So is the experience of tea. But it can be generally said that the stimulation of tea is a gentle one, that it invigorates rather than animates, and at the same time composes the mind and body with a feeling of relaxed refreshment. Extravagant claims of tea's curative powers may be true, but until they are proven, that is more than enough.

Herbal
Teas

Profit from Plants: The History of Herbs and Spices

Today as in the time of Pliny and Columella, the hyacinth flourishes in Wales, the periwinkle in Illyria, the daisy on the ruins of Numantia; while around them cities have changed their masters and their names, collided and smashed, disappeared into nothingness, their peaceful generations have crossed down the ages as fresh and smiling as on the days of battle.

—EDGAR QUINET (1803–1875)

Y ou don't have to be a horticulturist to know that flowers are beautiful, or a botanist to know that plants are valuable. And you certainly don't have to be an herbalist to make herbal teas. Before there was language, man was eating herbs—they were underfoot, after all, and hunger is a fine inspiration for adventurous eating. Combined with water, these plants became herbal teas, older by far than *Camellia sinensis* and with far wider growing fields. Where herbs grew and who harvested them has placed them at the vortex of history.

ASIAN ORIGINS

The recorded study and use of herbs began in the East. How the herbs themselves and their uses moved West is a mirror

119

of social, political, and economic events that span centuries. Chinese herbalism predates any other, and the man we have to thank is that same mythical emperor who found a tea leaf floating in his boiling water, Shen Nung. The *Pen T'sao Ching*, a compilation of 300 plants and their medicinal values, purported to be written around 3000 B.C., is attributed to him, although it is likely to have been codified in the second century A.D. No sense in quibbling about a few thousand years. The Chinese were first.

India was not far behind. The *Vedas*, ancient texts and legacy of Hindu gods, mention herbs as early as 2000 B.C. The Assyrians drank spiced wine, the ancient Egyptians embalmed their dead with herbs, and the Old Testament is fragrant with references to herbs and spices. By the time B.C. turned to A.D., hundreds of herbs and spices were used as remedies, in rituals, as oils, and as flavorings. Herbs went wherever man was going, and at that time, there was a lot of world to explore.

MIDDLE EASTERN MERCHANTS

If geography is destiny, the Middle East was the center of the universe in the early movement of herbs and spices. Arabs, consummate traders and masters of the roads between the East and Egypt, dominated the spice market from about 1500 B.C. to the sixteenth century. Mustard, dill, Chinese star anise, fennel, ginger, sesame, cinnamon, cloves, cardamom, and nutmeg, to name a few, traveled along a route that began in China, meandered through Ceylon, Malaysia, Burma, and crossed the Persian Gulf and the Red Sea from which the Arabs distributed their exotic wares.

GREEK SCHOLARSHIP

While the Arabs were profiting from herbs, the Greeks were studying them. In the first century A.D., a Greek physician, Dioscorides, made an impressive beginning in the annals of Western herbal scholarship with *De Materia Medica*, which describes 600 herbs and became a reference book for the next 1,500 years. When Alexander the Great rumbled his war machine into Alexandria in the fourth century, that city was already a center for herbs and spices. The Greeks recognized the value of these herbs. By the fourth century, Plato referred to herbal teas in his writings and Hippocrates, the West's fabled doctor, used herbal remedies.

ROMAN MIGRATION

The Romans, hedonists that they were, took everything a step further, even their herbs, bathing in lavender, sleeping on pillows of saffron, and anointing themselves with the perfume of flowers. After discovering the Arab routes to the East, over the next several centuries, the Romans were able to support their own herb and spice habit. And they took their herbs with them wherever they went. As the Roman Empire marched northward, conquering Europe and crossing into Britain, the seeds and roots of Mediterranean herbs and spices were planted by settlers along the way. Nature alone could never have been so ambitious. When the Romans were long gone, the plants remained. Their empire vanished, and history returned dominance of the spice trade to the Arabs.

In the mid-seventh century, under the influence of Mohammed and the rise of the Muslim religion, the Arab nations built their own empire, an enlightened civilization that lasted four centuries—and they held sway over the spice trade. Even during the eleventh, twelfth, and thirteenth centuries, when the Crusaders swept in from the West and the Turks from the East, the Arabs held their grip. They also planted herbs in their conquered territories, cultivating those that could tolerate northern climates in countries as far west as Spain. Herbs like coriander, fennel, cumin, caraway, and mustard took root and traveled throughout Europe and into Britain. Crusaders, returning from the Middle East, brought back herbs as seeds or on wounds dressed with herbal medicine. Herbal knowledge spread to Europe on the currents of history.

MUSLIM MIGHT

Europe, plunged into the Middle Ages, developed a taste for herbs to offset the unsavory nature of their food and to counteract very poor sanitary conditions. The demand was enough to enrich the city of Venice, which grew fat and prosperous as the main port of commerce with the East. Prices were high and, in self-defense, Europeans continued to grow their own, using herbs in cakes and puddings, soups and cheeses. Monasteries cultivated herbs and employed them for healing with chants and incantations. Physicians and sorcerers (a title innocent of today's connotations) prescribed herbal teas and made herb poultices, ointments, and oils to treat burns and bites and skin conditions. Some of their medical practices were barbaric, but some of their herbal medicine was prophetic.

TREASURE ISLANDS

In the fifteenth century, Europe came out of its long Medieval lethargy and set out to explore the world and play the spice traders' game. Portugal's Vasco da Gama pitched his ship around the Cape of Good Hope and became the first European to sail to India. Columbus embarked on his epic journey west to find the Spice Islands but found the rest of the world instead. The Portuguese, with their eye on the prize, were the first with a fleet to make the journey to the real Spice Islands, Indonesia and the Moluccas, and it made them rich. They were the envy of the rest of Europe.

SPICE WARS

But war was the only outcome of jealousy and greed on such a grand scale. By the end of the sixteenth century, the Age of Exploration put wind in the sails of Spain, England, and the Netherlands, all of whom were circumnavigating the globe, and not for the fun of it. The Dutch were the first to wrest the Spice Islands from Portugal, and they put their stamp on the territory with brutal force. At the end of the eighteenth century, England usurped Holland, pirates killed for a cargo of pepper, smugglers made fortunes in cloves, men lost their lives at sea, while herbs and spices orchestrated this traffic and mayhem. In the nineteenth century, the British turned to tea and relinquished their hold to the Dutch, who brought the spice trade into the beginning of the twentieth century.

Finally, the herbs and spices themselves made monopolies obsolete. During all that travel, the seeds gained a foothold and flourished in lands far from their origins. In the European colonization of North and South America alone, hundreds of species emigrated from the Old World to the New. Of course, herbs, like any plants, grow in certain climates, but the exclusivity of territory vanished for many. Today, if you have a garden or even a windowsill, you can begin your own herbal empire.

From Hippocrates to Poppies: Herbs as Medicine

The desire to take medicine is perhaps the greatest feature which distinguishes man from animals.

—SIR WILLIAM OSLER (1849–1919)

There are still many places in the world where herbal medicine is the *only* medicine. From the vantage point of a technological society, we would call it folk medicine. Because we take modern remedies in the form of pills, we have forgotten that, in the beginning, folk medicine and "real" medicine were inextricable, and plants were the heart of the matter. Western cultures tend to think of the East as the Herbal Kingdom, but herbalism is integral to the history of Western medicine. Even Hippocrates (c. 460–370 B.C.), the father of medicine, included over 400 simple herbal remedies in his writings.

MEDICINAL SHAPES AND HEAVEN-SENT HERBS

Not all early physicians were as sensible as Hippocrates. Paracelsus (1493–1541), a Swiss doctor, espoused a theory that must have developed from early folk beliefs. His work, *Herbal*, written in 1570, presented the Doctrine of Signatures, a practice so bizarre in retrospect that it is only worth mentioning because of the seriousness with which the people of his time took their herbs. According to this doctrine, the shape or property of an herb dictated its effect on man. In other words, if red juice could be extracted from a flower, that plant was perfect for treating wounds. Or if a plant lived among rocks, it should be used for gallstones. The mandrake root, which, with some imagination, looks like a sad-doll version of the human form, was recommended, of course, for general well-being.

At least Paracelsus's theory stuck to plants. Nicholas Culpeper, who wrote *The English Physician* in 1652, brought in the stars, mixing the zodiac and astrological signs with the fruit of the earth. According to his theory, a plant remedy might work if you were a Libra and Saturn was rising, but not if you were a Gemini and Jupiter was ascending. Embarrassed doctors of the day dismissed this marriage of plants and planets, but his book has been popular ever since.

TRANSATLANTIC TRANSFERS

Serious works, however, did prevail, and the gravity with which people took their herbs is evident in the need the first immigrants felt when striking out for the New World. The settlers took as many herbs with them as they could. At home in England, people cultivated their own herb gardens and many apothecaries and physicians grew herbs in their own ''physic'' gardens. People on both sides of the Atlantic were so interested in herbal remedies that settlers sent seeds back to the continent, too. In 1569, an Englishman in America, John Josselyn, wrote *New England's Rarities Discover'd*, detailing the botanicals he found in the Colonies. The British probably scoured his discoveries with the same eagerness that people today scan the newspapers for the latest up-to-date miracle cure. Faith in herbs is back.

PLANT PRINCIPALS AND MEDICAL PRACTICE

Modern science has proven herbal efficacy by creating some of our most useful and powerful drugs from the "principals" of plants. Until the 1800s, doctors using herbals struggled with the knowledge that the efficacy of plant leaves, stems, and flowers could not be regulated. Obviously, as all gardeners know, all plants of the same species are not created equal. Chemical research made it possible to extract a measured quantity of active principal, an isolated medicinal property, and to make it in exact doses. Plants may have many more than one active principal.

To say that this discovery made the difference between life and death to some people is not to exaggerate. At the very least, it relieved much disease and pain, two experiences most of us can never avoid entirely. Since these substances are now often taken for granted, here are a few to be grateful for:

Cocaine (Anesthetic)

From the coca leaf *(Erythroxylum coca)*, chewed by ancient Peruvians, scientists isolated the alkaloid cocaine in 1860. (An alkaloid is an organic compound.) It was the first local anesthetic. Consider your next dentist appointment without this discovery and, no doubt, its value will become clear.

Morphine (Painkiller)

The beautiful poppy *(Papaver somniferum)* gave us the first alkaloid to be isolated in the history of chemistry, in 1806, and that was opium from which morphine is made. There has never been a superior painkiller or a more addictive drug. Despite the problems the world has had with opium addiction, it is still the drug of choice for severe pain and terminal illness.

Quinine (Malaria Fighter)

Malaria has been fought with quinine, the active principal in cinchona bark (*Cinchona* species) since the seventeenth century. This disease is on the rise in the world again.

Reserpine (Tranquilizer)

Rauwolfia *(Rauvolfia serpentina)* was used to treat snakebite in India in the sixth century B.C. Perhaps tranquilizing the patient after the shock of meeting a cobra nose to nose was

all that could be done. Isolated since 1952, this drug has been beneficial in treating psychotic patients.

Aspirin, the World's Most Widely Used Drug

Let's not even think about the world without aspirin. But people did before 1899. Thank meadowsweet *(Filipendula ulmaria)* and the analgesic salicin which was first isolated from its leaves in 1827. It provided the basis for aceylsalicylic acid, called aspirin in 1899.

Mexican Yams (Oral Contraceptives)

Birth control pills have changed the sexual habits, social mores, and family planning practices of individuals all over the world. The Mexican yam (*Dioscorea* species) has made this revolution possible. Cortisone was isolated in this plant in 1934 and began an industry in steroidal drugs: corticosteroids, oral contraceptives, and sex hormones.

Green Thumbs and Dried Leaves: Personal Herbs

> *Behold I have given you every herb bearing seed which is upon the face of all the earth, and every tree, in which is the fruit of a tree yielding seed.*
>
> —GENESIS 1:29

Making herbal tea is a little like slipping into a candy store after hours and choosing whatever you crave, in any combination that entices you, with no proprietor, no scale, and not even the ghost of admonition in sight. Indulgence is the only rule. Simply choose an herb you think will please you, experiment, and try more.

To begin in a small way (sometimes the whole candy store is too much), buy herbal tea bags at a health food store or supermarket. This is not an adventurous foray and the quality of what you can buy will probably only give you a hint of what a freshly made cup of herbal tea is like. But try a few individual flavors to get a sense of what they are. Think of it as a first step, knowing that there is better to come.

Like growing your own. Growing herbs is not necessarily a burdensome gardening project. Small pots and windowsills will do. A square of land as big as a desk will yield more than you can use fresh. If you don't want to dry your herbs, eat them in your salad or season your soup, arrange them in a vase, or decorate your room. But the growing process is not difficult.

Start on a small scale with herbs that do well indoors like

angelica, basil, chamomile, dandelion, dill, horehound, lavender, lemon balm, mint, rosemary, sage, and thyme. Whether you buy plants or start from seeds depends entirely on your ambition and the greenness of your thumb. Place your herbs near a window where they will get maximum sun; a southern exposure is ideal. Artificial lights are a solution, if necessary. Harvest leaves, flowers, and stems whenever you want to enjoy them. Keeping an herb trimmed is like pruning a tree; it will grow fuller. Waiting too long may require traumatic cutting. That's all there is to it. If the season is right and your enthusiasm holds, the next step is to go outside to plant a small garden or head for the woods.

GOING WILD

The most authentic, back-to-nature approach to herbal teas is to gather herbs in the wild. Despite premature obituaries, and in the face of formidable concrete encroachment, nature is still alive and active. Herbs are a tenacious lot. Consider dandelions. Efforts to obliterate them to the contrary, they just keep coming. Might as well enjoy them. Harvesting from fields and forests is called *wildcrafting,* an activity that has all the pleasures and pitfalls you might expect. The satisfaction of going directly from nature to your cup is the best. But mistakes can be made, and there are herbs out there that are harmful, even poisonous. A good guidebook and an experienced companion are recommended before you brew anything whose every part is not 100 percent recognizable.

KEEPING THE CROP

If you want to keep herbs for later use, snip off the parts you want with scissors, and then preserve them by freezing or drying. Some herbs with delicate leaves, like basil or mint, freeze very well in plastic bags. Simply wash, dry, and freeze.

Drying herbs can be accomplished in a number of ways. Wash and dry them first, then try one of these methods.

Use your microwave at the lowest temperature for less than

a minute. The time varies, obviously, for ovens and herbs, so some trial and error is necessary.

The regular oven at a low heat, about 100° to 115°, is also an option. Spread the herbs on a rack with holes so air can circulate, leave the oven door open, and expect the whole process to be over in minutes. You don't want to bake out the essential oils.

The third method is air-drying. This can be done on racks or in paper bags with holes punched in. It's best to hang herbs upside down, if possible. If you're drying seeds, try the paper bag method, but don't punch holes in the bottom of the bag. When the herbs are dry, shake them in the bag, and the seeds should fall to the bottom.

Whatever the method, the outcome must be thoroughly brittle-dry herbs, which can be stored in airtight containers, like screw-top glass jars, in order to stay dry. Any moisture will cause mold. Store in a place that is cool and dry and preferably dark. Mark the herb containers with names, dates, and anything else that will help you remember what you thought you would recall. Although distinctly different when growing, many herbs look distressingly the same when dried. When you're brewing, you'll only want pleasant surprises.

Choosing the Brew: Herbs in Hot Water

> So hear it then, my Rennie dear,
>   Nor hear it with a frown;
> You cannot make the tea so fast
> As I can gulp it down.
>
> I therefore pray thee, Rennie dear,
>   That thou wilt give to me
> With cream and sugar softened well,
>   Another dish of tea.
>
> —DR. SAMUEL JOHNSON
> (1709–1784)

Brewing herbal tea is very personal, and therein lies its beauty. Individual taste necessarily negates rules, so what is provided here is the bare-bones melody of a jazz tune. You provide the rest of the song by making your herbal teas as singles or blends, mild or strong, tart or honeyed.

If you've been brewing tea *(Camellia sinesis),* you've got the tools: a teapot (nonmetallic), infuser, and strainer. Roots and seeds require a bit more basic paraphernalia. You'll need one more slightly violent utensil to grind them. Depending on your technological inclinations, that can be a wooden mallet wrapped in a cloth, a mortar and pestle, or a small coffee grinder. In addition to a kettle, you'll need an enamel or stainless steel pan for boiling water.

THE INFUSION

The process is the familiar one. Start with fresh, cold water. Bring it to a rolling boil in a kettle. Infuse the leaves in a pot or cup. Allow them to steep for about five minutes, or to the strength you prefer. If you are using an infuser, remove the plant parts. If the herb is loose in the pot, strain the tea into your cup. For one cup of boiling water, a suggested amount of leaves, petals, or flowers is one teaspoon of dried or three teaspoons of fresh. To get the most from the aromatic oils of the herb, try bruising the leaves (crushing them a bit in a towel) before infusing. The length of steeping, the amount of herb, and the strength of taste is truly subjective, so improvise until you're satisfied. In herbal parlance, this tea made by steeping is called an *infusion* or *tisane,* a French word.

THE DECOCTION

Herbs also are prepared as a *decoction,* which involves boiling instead of just steeping. Decoctions are, for the most part, made from roots and seeds that should be crushed or ground coarsely, or sometimes ground finely to a powder. The proportion of herb to water in this case is, again, not easily prescribed in a general way. The method is as follows: Place about one to two tablespoons of ground root or seed in an enamel or stainless steel pot. Cover with two cups of cold water. Bring to a boil, reduce heat, and simmer for ten to fifteen minutes or less, or until the liquid has been reduced by half. Depending on the strength desired, the herb can be removed immediately or be left in the liquid to cool and steep longer. Strain before using.

SIMPLING AND DOUBLING

Infusion or decoction, it's best to drink your concoction the day you make it. A tea with only one herb has the old-fashioned name, a *simple*—which doesn't mean that a simpleton makes it. When two or more herbs are combined, the drink is called by the sensible tea name, a *blend.* After you've been simpling for a while to get a sense of what each plant tastes like, try blending. More is not always better, but it may be, because personal preference is the only standard here. Just add herbs in equal parts and, if the result doesn't taste the way you had hoped, just acknowledge that it's not your cup of tea. A few commonly used blends of two are: chamomile and hibiscus flowers; elderflowers and peppermint; marigold petals and mint; and sage and lemon verbena.

There are probably as many herb combinations as there are lottery numbers, but any one you like is a winner. Go for three- and four-herb blends, grind up seeds and add them in equal parts for a decoction, mix and match dried and fresh herbs, and record your recipes, not only so that you can make them again, but because someday your grandchildren may regard them as venerable family treasures. Tea purists may scoff, but combining a touch of herb with regular tea can be a pleasant diversion of taste. Mint is especially good with green tea and lemon verbena is excellent with black tea. Tea is an inexpensive way to innovate.

Treating Oneself Well: Herbs for Health

Hail Queen of Plants, pride of Elysian bowers!
How shall we speak thy complicated Pow'rs?
Thou Wond'rous Panacea to asswage
The Calentures of Youth's fermenting rage,
And Animate the freezing Veins of age.

Thus our Tea-Conversation we employ
Where with Delight; Instruction we enjoy;
Quaffing, without the waste of Time or Wealth;
The Sov'reign Drink of Pleasure and of Health.

—NICHOLAS BRADY (1659–1726)

Herbs are everywhere, and defining them seems unnecessarily limiting. No matter what the definition, some plant that can be used to make an herbal tea will fail to be included. Narrowly, an herb is defined as a small, seed-bearing plant with fleshy rather than woody parts. But somehow, trees and shrubs, vines and ferns creep into any list of herbs. So, for present purposes, any plant that is used for its healthful properties and aromatic qualities is considered herbal.

WARNINGS

Although many people are skeptical about the health benefits of herbs, there is no question that plants contain medicinal properties. Their chemistry tells us so, but that does not mean that they are necessarily safe. Any herb can cause unpleasant reactions in some people. All are toxic if they are taken in excess. Some can cause unpredictable reactions when mixed with other herbs or medications. *The information here is intended for general interest only and should not be taken as a recommendation for use.* It should also be considered with these warnings:

Use herbal remedies only for minor complaints such as coughs or colds or upset stomachs. Think of herbs as improving health, not curing ailments.

Do not take herbal remedies with other medications, prescribed or over the counter, without checking with a qualified practitioner.

Pregnant women should not take herbal remedies. The effects may endanger the unborn child. Babies and elderly women should not take them unless they are prescribed by a qualified practitioner.

Herbal remedies prepared commercially, especially for diet formulas, tonics, and sedatives, often contain potent ingredients. Consult a qualified practitioner before using them.

POISONOUS PLANTS

The amount of toxicity in herbs varies, but even those often used in cooking like thyme and rosemary can be poisonous in excess, especially their essential oils, which are very volatile. The following herbs are considered poisonous:

Foxglove (*Digitalis* species)

Monkshoods (*Aconitum* species)

Meadow Saffron (*Colchicum* species)

Lily of the Valley *(Convallaria majalis)*

Opium Poppies *(Papaver somniferum)*

Pokeweeds (*Phytolacca* species)

Madagascar Periwinkle *(Catharanthuys roseus)*

Glory Lilies (*Gloriosa* species)

Castor Bean *(Ricinus communis)*

Variegated Nightshade *(Solanum dulcamara Variegatum)*

Daphnes (*Daphne* species)

HERBAL POSSIBILITIES

Keeping in mind that an herbal tea can be made by infusion or decoction out of practically anything, the following list is just a sampling. These herbs appear in compendiums that suggest the health benefits that are mentioned with each. None of them purport to be cures, and some have special warnings about length of use and use during pregnancy. Delving into herbs as medicine may seem strange to citizens of a technological age, but most are supported by long histories—in fact centuries—of use. Few, however, are backed by scientific evidence. Self-treatment with herbals is not a spectator sport. Your body is involved. Experiment cautiously, do not expect magic, and be open to the idea that you may very well enhance your health. At the very least, you will take an active role in doing something positive for yourself and that, in itself, is a health benefit.

Agrimony (Agrimonia eupatoria)

Because its burrs stick to clothing, this plant is also known as sticklewort and cocklebur, but its yellow flowers, which rise like spires, have also given it the more inspirational name, church steeples. It grows in fields and woods in Europe and North America. The early Anglo-Saxons believed agrimony would rescue them from goblins, evil, and poisons.

Use: Tea for coughs. Gargle for sore throat. It is also a good tonic.

To Brew: For an infusion, use two teaspoons of dried herb or three teaspoons of crushed, fresh in one cup of boiling water.

Angelica (Angelica archangelica)

Angelica's name is a clue to its origin. The legend is that an angel, perhaps even Michael, revealed the plant to a monk as a cure for plague. Indeed, it is also called St. Michael's Plant as well as Holy Ghost Plant. Those warding off the dread disease would have held the root in their mouths—a pacifier against plague. Angelica is also the name of a liqueur, and indeed, the seeds and an oil made from the stems and roots are used to flavor liqueurs like chartreuse, anisette, and some vermouths. The stems and leaves are also used to make candy. The tea is good with honey or lemon, especially for a cold.

Use: Tea for colds, flatulence, indigestion, and as a tonic.

To Brew: For an infusion, use one teaspoon of dried leaves or two to three teaspoons of fresh, crushed leaves for one cup of boiling water. For a decoction, pour two cups of boiling water over one tablespoon of crushed seeds or one ounce of crushed or ground root. Simmer at least five minutes.

Anise (Pimpinella anisum)

Also known as anise seed or aniseed, this plant is widely used as a flavoring in cakes and pastries. The ancient Egyptians used it, and the Romans never left it out of a wedding cake because they believed it was an aphrodisiac—as if newlyweds couldn't manage on their own. A whiff of anise, and you will know you've encountered the aroma before, not only in desserts, but in candies and liqueurs.

Use: Tea for nausea, indigestion, and flatulence. To encourage sleep, make the tea with hot milk instead of water, and strain. Take before bed.

To Brew: For an infusion, use one teaspoon of dried leaf or two to three teaspoons of fresh, crushed leaf for one cup of boiling water. For a decoction, pour two cups of boiling water over one teaspoon of crushed seeds. Simmer at least five minutes.

Balm or Lemon Balm (Melissa officinalis)

Balm is the sweetest of herbs. Thus it attracts bees and thus its Greek genus name, *Melissa,* which means *bee*. Introduced to England by the Romans, the British used it to collect bees for honey, as a surgical dressing, and even to polish furniture. Here is an herb for all seasons. With its pleasing odor, it is still used in perfumes and potpourri. In the kitchen, balm is used in some jellies and liqueurs. A refreshing summer drink is made from an infusion of the leaves, sugar, and lemon. Honey, sugar, and lemon can also be added to the hot infusion.

Use: For headaches, to reduce tension, and for sleep, make Melissa tea. Good for digestion after a meal and for settling the stomach from nausea.

To Brew: For an infusion, use one or two teaspoons of dried leaf or three to four teaspoons of fresh, chopped leaf for one cup of boiling water. Steep for at least ten minutes.

Bergamot (Monarda didyma)

Not the same as *Citrus bergamia,* which gives us the oil of bergamot that perfumes Earl Grey tea, this bergamot is a native North American herb. The Oswego Indians brewed the leaf before the Pilgrims arrived, and the early settlers made bergamot tea when the Boston Tea Party suspended their use of the real thing. A member of the mint family, it is also called mountain mint and bee balm. Try it in combination with regular tea for an interesting taste.

Use: For inducing sleep, bergamot makes a good sedative.

To Brew: For an infusion, use two teaspoons of dried leaves or flowers for one cup of boiling water. To make bergamot milk, to be taken just before bed, pour a cup of boiling milk over two to three teaspoons of fresh or dried leaves.

Borage (Sanguisorba officianilis)

"Borage for courage" is an old saying probably stemming from a belief of the ancient Greeks, who put it in their wine to rally their spirits. As part of that legacy, the plant remains a symbol of courage. An herb with lovely flowers that look like five-pointed azure stars, borage has a smell similar to cucumbers.

Use: For lifting mild depression and reducing fever.

To Brew: For an infusion, use two teaspoons of dried or fresh leaves or flowers for one cup of boiling water. Simmer gently, remove from heat, and allow to steep a few minutes. Strain. It is best to crush the fresh herb.

Chamomile (Anthemis noblis)

This plant's name is derived from the Greek meaning *earth apple* because its scent is reminiscent of apples. Another name, *manzanilla,* for *little apples* in Spanish, is taken from a Spanish wine flavored with chamomile. The flowers are the part of the chamomile plant that are used in making tea. The herb is so popular that tea bags and loose flowers for tea can readily be purchased in drugstores and supermarkets.

Use: Chamomile settles the stomach and acts on digestion and flatulence.

To Brew: For an infusion, use two teaspoons of dried flowers or one tablespoon of fresh in a cup of boiling water. Steep for fifteen minutes. Strain. For fevers, use a stronger infusion, about two tablespoons in a cup of boiling water. Let steep for at least thirty minutes and cool. Drink cold with honey and/or lemon.

Coltsfoot (Tussilago farfara)

The generic name of coltsfoot hints at its use. *Tussis* is Latin for cough, and thus the herb is said to be a remedy for coughs and hoarseness. It is also an herbal tobacco smoked in pipes and as cigarettes. The smoke has been used, at various times in history, to relieve asthma sufferers. The plant resembles a small dandelion on a purplish stalk, and because of its shape, it is also called horsehoof or horsefoot. Coltsfoot has a sharp, bitter taste and is best accompanied by honey.

Use: Coltsfoot contains vitamin C in both its leaves and flowers and thus makes a good tonic. It is used as an infusion for coughs and hoarseness.

To Brew: For an infusion, use one teaspoon of dried or two teaspoons of fresh leaves and flowers in a cup of boiling water. Steep for ten minutes. Strain. Sweeten with honey. To make a decoction for coughs or hoarseness, use one to two tablespoons of dried leaves or flowers to two cups of boiling water. Boil down to half. Strain. Sweeten with honey.

Dandelion (Taraxacum officinale)

If dandelions are rampant in your lawn, the best course of action is to dig them up and eat them. The leaves make a tasty salad, a cooked vegetable, or even a soup. Or make dandelion wine. Dandelion is the incredible edible. To someone who was more interested in the plant's shape than its taste, the dandelion's leaves looked like lion's teeth. Thus, the plant got its name, from the French *dent de lion.* Well endowed with potassium and calcium and high in vitamin A, dandelion tea makes a fine tonic. It's bitter, so add honey. If using fresh leaves, choose the youngest possible.

Use: As an infusion or decoction, use dandelion for constipation and as a tonic. Take regularly for results.

To Brew: For an infusion, use one teaspoon dried leaves or two to three teaspoons fresh with a cup of boiling water. Infuse for ten minutes. Strain. Use with honey. For a decoction, cover two to three teaspoons of leaves with one cup of cold water in a pot. Bring to boil and boil briefly. Allow to stand for fifteen minutes. Strain.

Dill (Anethum graveolens)

If you love pickles, you know the taste of dill. Used in pickling cucumbers, in soups, and to season many foods, this plant with the feathery leaves is a familiar kitchen herb. Its name is derived from the Saxon word *dilla,* which means *to lull,* an indication of its sleep-inducing qualities. A decoction made with the seeds is the strongest method of using the herb, but an infusion can also be made with the leaves.

Use: An infusion or decoction is good for the digestion, for flatulence, and as a sedative.

To Brew: For a decoction, place two teaspoons of crushed dill seeds in a pot with one cup of water. Bring to a boil and simmer for ten to fifteen minutes. Let stand for an equal amount of time. Strain. Sweeten with honey. For an infusion, pour one cup of boiling water over one teaspoon of dried or two to three teaspoons of crushed fresh leaves. Steep for at least five minutes or to taste. Strain. Sweeten with honey.

Elder (Sambucus nigra)

Also known as elderberry or elderflower, this plant was so widely used in seventeenth-century England that an entire book, *The Antomie of the Elder*, was devoted to the "medicine chest of the country people." In addition, elder is a tree with good luck/bad luck properties—good to have around to ward off evil spirits, but bad to cut down or burn. Working with the flowers to make a tea seems to be the best bet.

Use: An infusion is good for colds, sore throats, and headaches.

To Brew: Use two tablespoons of fresh or dried flowers for one cup of boiling water. Infuse for ten minutes or to taste. Strain. Add honey if desired.

Ginseng (Panax quinquefolium) North American; (Panax ginseng) Asian

It's almost too much to imagine that Shen Nung, the emperor who brought tea to the world, is also the man who discovered ginseng, but that's the way the story goes. Ginseng has been credited over the last 5,000 years with fixing just about everything that ails you. One of its other names, man root, is a hint that it has been considered an aphrodisiac and sexual rejuvenator for several of those thousands of years. The Chinese do know their herbs, and ginseng is given a great deal of credibility as general tonic and strength builder.

Use: Tonic for general health. Ginseng can be bought in health food stores as a root, a powder, or a pill.

To Brew: The tea can be made from the ground root using one teaspoon of powdered ginseng to two cups of boiling water. Simmer for fifteen minutes.

Ginger (Zingiber officinale)

In Indian Ayurvedic medicine, ginger is known as the universal medicine. The Chinese would agree. They've been using it since A.D. 25, and the Romans were not far behind. Anyone who's ever eaten gingerbread understands its culinary popularity, and that's been going on a long while—the ancient Egyptians were the first to make it. The rather gnarled and twisted root once inspired ginger's inclusion in the *Doctrine of Signatures*. Said to resemble the human intestines, it was used for digestion. For once, the *Doctrine* was right.

Use: Ginger is the secret weapon against motion sickness. It follows that it would be appropriate for nausea and digestion. Ginger is also used for colds and coughs.

To Brew: Grind the root for fresh herb or use powdered. For an infusion, use one teaspoon dried or two teaspoons fresh to one cup of boiling water.

Hawthorn (Crataegus species)

There are many varieties of hawthorn shrubs and trees, but they are all a hardwood and are close relatives to the apple. Indeed, among hawthorn's other names are mayblossom and thornapple. Perhaps the strength of the wood is what inspired the Pilgrims to name the *Mayflower* after this plant. For all its hardness, hawthorn, as a decoction from the berries or a tea made from the flowers, has a gentle, calming effect.

Use: To relieve tension and promote sleep.

To Brew: For a decoction, crush two teaspoons of dried berries and cover with one cup of water. Allow to soak for eight hours or overnight, bring to a boil, and remove from heat. Strain. Sweeten with honey. For an infusion, use two teaspoons of flowers to one cup of boiling water. Steep for ten minutes or to taste. Strain. Sweeten with honey.

Hops (Humulus lupulus)

The hop has been used since the 1300s to make one century or another's version of beer, mead, or ale. The Spanish have the best name, *flores de cerveza,* with means *flowers of beer.* The female cones are the beloved part used in the process of brewing. Both the female flowers and the leaves have herbal medicinal content. Not surprisingly, hops is an herb that aids sleeping.

Use: To induce sleep or as a general tonic.

To Brew: For an infusion, use one teaspoon of dried leaves or two to three teaspoons of fresh, crushed, leaves with one cup of boiling water. Steep for ten minutes. Strain. Drink before bed. For a decoction, steep one to two tablespoons of female cones (flowers) in two cups of boiling water. Bring to a boil and simmer five minutes. Strain.

Horehound (Marrubium vulgare)

Horehound is one of those herbs that smells better than it tastes. Its bitterness is best offset by honey. The plant was known and respected by the ancient Egyptians, who called it seed of Horus, a powerful god. Most of the ancient belief in this herb's magical powers has come down to cough drops in modern times—but very good cough drops. It follows that horehound's effectiveness as a tea is in relation to colds and coughs.

Use: For colds, especially head colds and coughs, particularly if the chest is congested.

To Brew: For an infusion, use one teaspoon of dried leaves or two to three teaspoons of fresh, crushed, to one cup of boiling water. Steep ten minutes. Strain. Drink as hot as possible.

Hyssop (Hyssopus officinalis)

"Purge me with hyssop and I shall be clean; wash me, and I shall be whiter than snow." These were the words of King David in the Old Testament, and they provide ample evidence that hyssop was the herbal symbol of purification from sin. It is also called the sacred herb. Today, most of the cleansing that hyssop does involves the chest in coughs and colds.

Use: For coughs and colds, especially to relieve tightness and congestion in the chest. Also may help to reduce fever during flu.

To Brew: For an infusion, use one teaspoon of dried hyssop flowers to one cup of boiling water. Steep for ten minutes. Strain. Sweeten with honey. This treatment, which can be taken twice a day, should not continue longer than two weeks. A decoction of hyssop is used externally. It is not for drinking.

Lavender (Lavandula spica, L. vera, *and other species)*

Lavender's sweet scent wafts through the centuries, eclipsing the beauty of this lovely plant. The Romans, who knew how to live well, put lavender in their baths and the twelveth-century English made lavender water one of their earliest perfumes. The scent has not lost its attraction over time. Lavender soap and lavender oil are still popular.

Use: Lavender is one of the main herbs used for headache. It is good for relieving nervousness. It works for sleep and against dizziness.

To Brew: For an infusion, use one teaspoon of dried or two to three teaspoons of fresh flowers to one cup of boiling water. Cover, and infuse for ten minutes. Strain.

Lemon Verbena (Lippia citriodora *or* Aloysia triphylla)

Lemon verbena is native to Chile and Peru, but in the eighteenth century, it crossed the Atlantic to Europe and now crops up in places as far apart as India and North America. Its name is transformed as it travels. In France it is *vervain*. In Spain, the plant is called *yerba Luisa.* Its pleasant lemony taste and smell make this herb an ideal candidate for a palatable tea. Indeed, it is delicious and refreshing as iced tea, sweetened with honey.

Use: For indigestion. Also used to reduce tension and induce sleep.

To Brew: Use one teaspoon dried leaves or two to three teaspoons fresh leaves to one cup of boiling water. Infuse for five to ten minutes. Strain. Sweeten with honey. Take before bed for sleep.

Lime Flower or Linden (Tilia europaea *and other species*)

One of the best-loved herbal teas is made with the flowers of this tree, which can grow to ten feet high. Popular in North America and Europe, it is used as an after-dinner drink called *tilleul* in France. The tree is also called basswood, and its fine, soft wood is popular for carving. The smell alone is soothing, and the tea has a calming, sleep-inducing effect.

Use: To bring down fever; to reduce tension by calming the nerves; and to encourage sleep.

To Brew: Use two teaspoons of dried or fresh flowers to one cup of boiling water. Infuse for five minutes. Strain. Sweeten with honey, if desired.

Mint (Mentha *and other species*)

The mint varieties include garden mint (spearmint), peppermint, apple mint, orange mint, and hundreds of others. Peppermint *(Menta piperita)* wins as the mint with the best myth of origin, a soap opera of infidelity, revenge, and resurrection. The Greek story goes that Persephone discovered the nymph Minthe with her husband Pluto. Not one to turn the other cheek, the enraged goddess attacked the nymph, crushing her beneath her foot. A remorseful Pluto managed to transform his little lover into a plant as sweet in leaves as she was in life. We are all the beneficiaries. Used in cooking and scenting by the ancient Romans and Greeks, it wasn't until the eighteenth century that peppermint was used for its considerable medicinal qualities.

Use: Good for a calming effect on digestive upsets and flatulence. Also calms nervous tension and stress.

To Brew: Use one to two teaspoons of dried leaves or two to three teaspoons of crushed fresh leaves to a cup of boiling water. Steep for ten minutes. Strain. Sweeten with honey, if desired.

Nettle (Urtica dioica)

Known as stinging nettle because the entire plant is blanketed with stinging hairs, nettle has been all things to all people over the centuries. Nettle soup, nettle porridge, and nettle beer are just a few of the ingenious uses people have put this plant to. It's been claimed to cure everything from sciatica to inflammations of all kinds. Probably its greatest claim to fame is nettle cloth, a material common in the nineteenth century. And that's not all; it was used for ropes, sailcloth, nets for fishing fleets, and even paper. Most of these uses overlooked its precious high vitamin content, which makes nettle tea a very good tonic.

Use: Good for overall tonic, especially for its vitamin C content.

To Brew: Pour one cup of boiling water over one to two teaspoons of dry leaves. Steep ten minutes. Strain.

Rose (Rosa *species*)

Evidence of a rose was found in the grave of a Sumerian king buried 5,000 years ago. Roses have been around for a very long time. Nearly every civilization since then has extolled the rose for its beauty and perfume—and taste, too, for roses have been used in cooking for centuries. Today, roses appear as flavoring in cough syrups and medicines, and their fruit extracts are added to vitamin C tablets. Rose oil is used as a component in almost all women's perfumes and nearly half of men's colognes. With over 10,000 varieties, roses are almost too beautiful to think of as herbal, but the petals and particularly the hips, the fruit under the wilted flower, have high concentrations of vitamins, especially vitamin C. A cup of hips are purported to have as much vitamin C as 150 oranges.

Use: For those who believe in the efficacy of vitamin C to ward off colds, rose tea is a very good source. Its vitamin content may also make rose an effective tonic.

To Brew: Pour one cup of boiling water over one teaspoon dried or two to three teaspoons fresh petals. Steep for five minutes or to taste. Ground dry hips may be used in the proportions of one teaspoon to one cup of boiling water.

Rosemary (Rosmarinus officinalis)

Rosemary is the herb of remembrance and fidelity, which historically placed a sprig at gravesides and in bridal bouquets. An ancient plant, its virtues have been extolled for everything from beautifying hair to alleviating hangovers. In the sixteenth century, William Langham wrote in *The Garden of Health*, "Seethe much rosemary, and bathe therein to make thee lusty, lively, joyfull, likeing and youngly." Not a bad recommendation. Today, we may look to rosemary for relief from headaches and depression.

Use: For headaches and depression. Should not be used by pregnant women. Do not take for prolonged periods of time.

To Brew: To infuse flowers, pour one cup of boiling water over one teaspoon of dried flowers or two to three teaspoons of fresh. Steep for five to ten minutes or to taste. Sweeten with honey. For a strong infusion, use leaves. Pour one cup of boiling water over half teaspoon of dried leaves or one teaspoon of fresh. Steep for five to ten minutes or to taste. Sweeten with honey.

Sage (Salvia officinalis)

Known as *salvia salvatrix,* or *sage the savior,* sage has a reputation for prolonging life. It is also an ancient symbol of wisdom, which means that taking sage would make one both aged and wise, a double prize. There are over 700 varieties, all rich in volatile oils that produce a broad spectrum of aromas. From the ancient Chinese forward, sage seems to have been used to strengthen several parts of the body. The Greeks regarded the herb as a brain booster, the Egyptians as a fertility enhancer. In the Middle Ages it was used to ward off plague. All that and this, too: Thanksgiving turkey would not be the same without sage in the stuffing.

Use: For indigestion, especially after a rich meal. Regular use for more than two weeks is not recommended. Also may be effective for headaches.

To Brew: Pour one cup of boiling water over one teaspoon of dried or chopped fresh leaves. Steep for five to ten minutes. Strain. Sweeten with honey.

Thyme (Thymus vulgaris)

Walk into an Italian restaurant and you will be at home with thyme, one of the common ingredients in an herb-rich tomato sauce. The ancient Greeks used this aroma as an incense to scent their homes and drive out insects. The name, pronounced *time*, means *fumigate* in Greek. Indeed, the plant is used today as part of moth-repelling sachets. In addition to its medicinal uses for indigestion and diarrhea, thyme is found in mouthwashes and toothpastes.

Use: Good for indigestion, diarrhea, and flatulence. Should not be taken by pregnant women.

To Brew: Pour one cup of boiling water over one teaspoon dried leaves or two to three teaspoons of crushed fresh leaves. Steep for five to ten minutes. Strain. Sweeten with honey.

Valerian (Valeriana officinalis)

Valerian is also called garden heliotrope and phu, a name it may have acquired because of its unpleasant odor—to humans, that is. Rats, however, seem to be attracted to valerian, and so there is speculation that the herb was the Pied Piper of Hamelin's secret weapon when he paraded the rat population out of town. As long ago as the tenth century the plant received its name from the Latin, meaning *to be well*. Its most general use is for insomnia.

Use: Good for sleeplessness. Valerian tea should not be taken too strong or for too long or the opposite effect may occur, causing restlessness and headache rather than relaxation. Two weeks is the maximum.

To Brew: For an infusion, pour one cup of boiling water over a half teaspoon of ground, dried valerian root. Steep for at least ten minutes. Strain. The taste is not appealing, so definitely sweeten with honey. The tea should always be taken cold. For a decoction, grate a teaspoon of dried root. Place in a bowl with one cup of cold water, cover, and let stand overnight. Strain.

AILMENTS AND HERBS

As a reference, the herbs listed above may be effective for the following ailments:

Colds: angelica, coltsfoot, elderflower, ginger, horehound, hyssop, lime flower (linden), rose hips

Constipation: dandelion

Coughs: agrimony, coltsfoot, elderflower, ginger, horehound, hyssop

Depression: borage, rosemary

Diarrhea: thyme

Dizziness: lavender, lemon balm

Fever: borage, chamomile, hyssop, lime flower (linden)

Flatulence: angelica, anise, chamomile, dill, lemon balm, peppermint, thyme

Headache: elderflower, lavender, lemon balm, rosemary, sage

Indigestion: angelia, anise, chamomile, dill, ginger, lemon balm, lemon verbena, peppermint, sage, thyme

Insomnia: anise, bergamot, chamomile, dill, hawthorn, hops, lavender, lemon balm, lemon verbena, lime flower (linden), valerian

Nausea: anise, ginger, lemon balm

Sore throat: coltsfoot, edlerflower, horehound, hyssop, sage

Tension: hawthorn, lavender, lemon balm, lemon verbena, lime flower (linden), peppermint

Tonic (overall strengthening effect): agrimony, angelica, coltsfoot, dandelion, ginseng, hops, nettle, rose

Tea Ceremonies: Ancient and One's Own

Nations Take Tea:
No Place Like Home

I am a hardened and shameless tea-drinker, who has, for twenty years, diluted his meals with only the infusion of this fascinating plant; whose kettle has scarcely time to cool; who with tea amuses the evening, with tea solaces the midnight, and, with tea, welcomes the morning.

—DR. SAMUEL JOHNSON (1709–1784)

Yak butter in your tea? Or jam, perhaps? Or mint or cardamom? It all depends on where you take your tea—and that can be almost anywhere. Tea is international. The world of tea was a global village long before telecommunications gathered us all around a network campfire. China, Japan, and England are the tea Meccas, of course, but there are many other peoples whose lives would be inconceivable without tea.

IRANIAN FLORALS

The Iranians, for example, are a nation of tea drinkers—*hourly* tea drinkers. Although breakfast is the only meal at which tea is served, a hot cup of tea is everyone's companion the day long. Evening guests served tea inhale the aroma of scented flower blossoms and herbs, which the Iranians use to flavor their tea leaves.

MOROCCAN MINT

Mint is the preference of Moroccans, who were not introduced to tea until the middle of the nineteenth century, but who then embraced it with a passion. Tea in Morocco is green, the sprigs of mint are fresh, and the drink is always sweet, for sugar is added to the pot, never to the cup. Politeness in this culture demands that anyone who accepts one glass of tea takes two more, and, of course, no one is ever rude under the civilizing influence of tea.

RUSSIAN SAMOVARS

While the Moroccans pour their tea from silver or brass pots, the Russians, to satisfy their generous appetite for tea, traditionally use a samovar, a large charcoal-fired copper urn that heats up to forty cups of water at one time. The actual tea is brewed in a teapot, which is kept warm on the saucer-shaped crown of the samovar. This traditional way of taking tea dates back to the time when tea from China, shaped into bricks, came to Russia by caravan through Manchuria and Mongolia, a trip of 11,000 miles made with over 200 camels that took sixteen months to complete. It was then called Russian tea, a name that appears in tea blends today. Russian tea is held in glasses cradled in silver holders. It is one-quarter tea essence from the pot and three-quarters water from the samovar. Lemon is optional, milk is never served, and sugar is added in a uniquely Russian manner: A lump is held between the teeth, and the tea is sipped through the sugar. Jam is sometimes swirled into the tea as another way of sweetening, and a jolt of liquor is not unheard of to fortify drinkers against the formidable Russian weather.

INDIAN *CHAI*

Even in hot climates, people drink hot tea, and India, a tea-growing nation, is first among them. Tea is not native to the Hindu culture but was brought to the country by the British who, as a colonial power, developed the tea industry and left the imprint of their customs on the native people. In the cities, tea is taken in the British manner with lemon, milk, and sugar as accompaniments. But throughout the countryside, *chai* is flavored with a more indigenous touch. Tea leaves are boiled in water in an open pot, cardamom seeds are added, or sometimes cinnamon or even ginger, and then sugar and milk. Everywhere in India, in tea establishments, in railway stations, on the side of the road, vendors sell this sweet, milky brew.

SRI LANKAN TEA BOUTIQUES

Sri Lanka, formerly Ceylon, is another of the large tea-producing nations that adopted tea as a national drink. The British left their mark here, too, and urban Sri Lankans take their tea as the English do, with complete china tea service when they can. They take it even a bit farther, with tea at breakfast, midmorning, midafternoon, and often before bed. In the villages, tea is a social affair served in tea boutiques, which are identified by a bunch of bananas hanging over the door. These serve as a Southeast Asian equivalent of the Irish pub, an oasis where workers gather on their way home to sip tea, chew a bit of betel leaf, and ease the strains of the day.

AUSTRALIAN BILLY

Far from the tea-growing nations of the world, Australians, renegade descendants of the English, carry on their tea customs Down Under. Mavericks that they are, Australian outbackers, those that travel the far reaches of their vast country, have the most casual of tea rituals. It begins with the *billy,* the prized tin can hanging on a stick over an open fire that all campers use to boil water. Tea leaves are added to the billy and boiled—and boiled—to a very strong drink, sipped in the morning, simmered all day, and drunk again at night. If the billy sounds familiar, think of the song, "Waltzing Matilda." The *matilda* is the inexplicably named knapsack carried by outbackers, and so the song goes, "And he sang as he watch'd and waited till his billy boil'd/'You'll come a-waltzing Matilda with me.' " Tea goes everywhere.

TIBETAN YAK BUTTER

Tea has even reached the top of the world, where Tibetans civilize life in the frozen Himalayas with a hot cup of tea. Strong and steeped for an hour, Tibetan tea does not resemble the clear amber or green drink sipped by English queens and Japanese emperors. Quantities of salt are added to the tea. It is then churned with butter made from the milk of a yak, the mountains' long-haired beast of burden. The smell is not delicate, the color is muddied with butterfat, but it is tea—body-warming, soul-embracing tea.

The Chinese Tea Ceremony: The Spirit of Kung Fu

Tea urges tranquillity of the soul.

—WILLIAM WORDSWORTH LONGFELLOW (1807–1882)

The Chinese approach tea with a carefree spirit. If there is an art to the Chinese tea ceremony, it is the ideal of pleasure in a distilled moment of relaxation. There are no rules in Chinese tea, yet their procedure is called *kung fu,* which means *skill and practice* or *patient effort,* which sounds suspiciously like knowledge and work. But that would be wrong. Chinese tea is all about pleasure within an informal framework, a loose structure that provides sanctuary from the stresses of the day. It has form without rigidity, artfulness without self-consciousness. It is a routine in which the familiar steps offer the soothing satisfaction of fulfilled expectations

The perfect Chinese tea has five basics that are meant to mesh harmoniously: *setting, company, tea, water,* and *tea things.* None of these have strict requirements. In a perfect world, the setting would be serene, restful, and close to nature. There was a time when the Chinese elite erected small buildings, teahouses, adjacent to their homes and landscaped with a pond and garden designed to reflect the poetic feeling of drinking tea. But any comfortable setting will do, for the place is not as important as the feeling—and the company. Tea is not for casts of thousands but for the few, two or three congenial friends. Of course, tea must be served to guests and business associates and even strangers. Nonetheless, the ceremony and the tea itself, when served with respect and appreciation, are still a great pleasure.

Only one rule stands for choosing a tea: select whatever you like that is the best you can afford. Traditionally, oolongs are used for the kung fu ceremony and the brew takes some getting used to. Sipped from tiny cups, the traditional drink is strong and bitter and must be savored more like brandy than tea. The perfect brewing water, which is high in minerals, low in chemicals, and free of odor, is still hard to come by even though time and plumbing have erased the problem of searching mountain streams as Lu Yü suggested in *The Classic of Tea.*

TEA THINGS

The tea things for kung fu tea all have ancient originals of considerable beauty. But the implements are not the point, the moment of tea is, so the only criteria are that the utensils are not ugly and that they look well together. When the components mingle with simple grace, the experience of Chinese tea achieves a harmony that is more than the sum of its parts. The parts, which follow, may not seem so simple at first, but in fact, they are quite utilitarian, perfectly designed for their function. Most are a legacy of the Sung Dynasty.

A teapot: Here there is a rule. The teapot should be earthenware, and the best are the clay pots from the famous Yixing (pronounced *E-shing*) region of China. These pots are unglazed and need to be seasoned by boiling them in a pan filled with water and old tea leaves for about three hours. The beauty of these pots lies in the clay and the porous inner surfaces, which absorb tea fragrances. They should never be scoured, but only rinsed with clean water. The surprise is their size—no bigger than a tangerine. A **tea boat** goes with the pot. This is a small bowl to rest the pot in. Its sides should reach about halfway up the teapot.

A portable charcoal stove: Not likely today, perhaps, but traditionally, these tea stoves were used as the most aesthetic and odor-free means of boiling water. Much was made of the commingling of fire and water, the beauty of the red-glowing charcoal and the crackling of the fire as contributing to the atmosphere of the tea ceremony. Any means of boiling water will do, of course, but gas stoves are said to be avoided because of the odor. Fine tea is believed to be extremely susceptible to contamination by odors, a reason why the tea ceremony is not supposed to take place in the kitchen where a cooking aroma may waft by.

A kettle and a small stand to place it on when it is hot.

A caddy, an airtight container for tea, traditionally silver or porcelain.

Three or four tiny, handleless cups: They may be earthenware, but white porcelain, or at least, a white inner surface, is preferred so that the color of the tea can be observed. These are placed on a **cup plate,** a round, flat plate with a rim to keep the cups from sliding off. Basically, it serves as a tray to pass the cups to guests.

A small tray, holding a **tea cloth** and a **spoon** used to scoop tea from the caddy.

A tea plate: This is the only object that needs explaining, but once its function is clear, it's easy to picture. Imagine a two-tiered tray somewhat like a broiler pan only made of ceramic. The top has symmetrically placed holes because, during the tea ceremony, water is going to pour through these holes and collect in the bottom. The tea plate is big enough so that the teapot and small cups can sit on its surface.

A jug, a bucket, a vessel of some type that can be placed on the floor and do the job of holding excess water if a tea plate isn't available. In keeping with the tea ceremony, it can't be ugly, so this is a place for clever improvisation.

A broken fan: There *is* an explanation. Traditionally, a rattan fan was used to revive the fire. The broken part is in regard to an ancient Chinese belief that "Nothing can be perfect unless it includes one tiny imperfection." (The imperfection in your Chinese tea ceremony may be that you have no fan.)

A tea table: The Chinese used lacquered wooden tables that were impervious to water. Expect to spill some hot water in the beginning, and choose a place accordingly.

FLOOR PLAN

For a ceremony that claims to have no rules, the Chinese tea ceremony does have arrangements. Where all these implements stand matters. Picture this: The host sits at one end of the table. The kettle, the stove, and the fan are to his right, on the floor. The vessel for collecting water, if used, is on the floor to his left. The tea plate is on the table in front of him. Resting on the tea plate are the teapot, sitting prettily in its tea boat, and the little cups. On the table, beyond the tea plate, is the cup plate. To the right, on the table, is the tea caddy, and on the left is the small tray with the tea cloth and spoon. Guests are seated around the table.

TEA TIMING

Go. The water boils in the kettle. The teapot is scalded inside and out with hot water to raise its temperature. Water is poured into the teapot until it cascades over and fills the tea boat. A few seconds later, the water in the teapot and the tea boat is poured through the holes in the tea plate where it collects in the bottom.

Tea leaves—a lot—are spooned from the caddy into the teapot. If oolong is used, the pot is half filled with leaves; if green tea is used, about one-third is filled. Hot water is poured from the kettle into the pot, again filling the teapot and the tea boat. Note: the water is not poured in one stream into the middle of the leaves, but is circled so that all the leaves are moistened. The lid is placed on the pot. Then the water is immediately poured out into the tea plate. This quick rinse infusion is called *washing the leaves*.

The pot is refilled, the lid returned, and more scalding water poured over the pot. The tea steeps for about thirty seconds. The cups are scalded by pouring water over them. The cups are placed very closely, side by side, like little soldiers, on the cup plate. The tea is poured into them in a continuous stream, filling each one halfway and then filling each all the way in reverse order, so all have tea of the same strength.

Everyone *sips* their tea (even though it is only a shot glass full) and savors the flavor and fragrance. The empty cups are returned. Immediately, another infusion is made with water from the still-hot kettle. At least three more infusions follow. The steeping time increases a bit with each. And each cup is different, offering altered intensities of flavor, nuances, subtleties, and deeper refreshment.

There is no doubt that this refreshment goes beyond the physical, but practitioners of kung fu tea would not claim that the *purpose* of the ceremony is spiritual. Yet, developed by scholars and poets, Chinese tea *is* an art, and like any art form, it's an expression of the human spirit aspiring to beauty in everyday life. In order to experience tea in this way, one comes to it with an attitude of "mindfulness" or what the Buddhists call "awareness." All the senses are engaged in giving attention to the bubble of the boiling water, the harmonious whole of the implements, the fragrance and taste of the brew, and the pleasantness of the surroundings. No thoughts of the past or future intrude, and only the present exists for the moment. If this oasis of the mind brings an unexplained elation, a heightened exhilaration that cannot be explained in words, then, in this sense, Chinese tea is spiritual.

The Japanese Tea Ceremony: Ritual and Aesthetics

More grace than possessed was needed
As the ceremony quaint proceeded,
But—at length—we sipped the bowl
Where east and west with disparate soul
Do meet, for all the world drinks tea.

—ANTOINETTE ROTAN PETERSON,
FROM "THE OLD TEA MASTER OF KYOTO"

The Japanese tea ceremony is not so much about tea as it is about ceremony. A stylized ritual in which every motion is choreographed, the ceremony is not an end in itself but a vehicle in which the participants seek peacefulness through a bowl of tea. *Chado,* or the Way of Tea, was originated in Japan by monks who visited Zen Buddhist monasteries in southern China in the twelfth century. Inspired by the Chinese monks' practice of sharing a worshipful bowl of tea before an image of Bodhidharma, they developed their own version. *Chanoyu,* the Japanese ceremonial drinking of tea, is the result. The old Chinese monks would have been shocked.

The *Rules for the Tea Ceremony*, of which there are many more than the Ten Commandments, were set down by the tea master of all time, Sen-no Rikyu (1521–1591), who was also responsible for establishing the architectural uniqueness of the tea house and garden. Both are physical aspects of the Zen philosophy, spare and natural, yet studiously arranged in a kind of austere purity.

THE SETTING

To set the stage: The teahouse has an entranceway, which is in itself a small room where guests gather; a small kitchenlike preparation room, and a main room with a place for each person to kneel on a *tatami,* a three-foot-by-six-foot straw mat. In addition, there is an alcove for displaying two essential pieces of art, a *chabana,* a flower arrangement, and a *kakemono,* a hanging scroll.

The utensils are carefully selected to be in harmony with one another but at the same time not to be repetitious in design. Okakura Kakuzo (1862–1913) explains in *The Book of Tea* that everything in the room should adhere to the Japanese principle of asymmetry; a round kettle would be countered with an angular water pitcher, and no object would rest exactly in the center of its display place, "in order to break any suggestion of monotony in the room." The entire ceremony and its surroundings are intended to be a work of art, and they are.

Indeed, *chanoyu* has played an important role in the artistic life of the Japanese. As an aesthetic pursuit, the tea ceremony involves the appreciation of architecture, decor, furnishings, flower arranging, landscaping, and ceramics. All these aspects of Japanese culture have been influenced by the studied simplicity and harmony with nature inherent in the tea ceremony. And the formalities observed in the tea ceremony have influenced the development of the manners of the Japanese in a fundamental way.

THE CEREMONY

The Japanese Tea Ceremony is for one guest or two, five or six, but rarely more. The original was an affair that lasted two and a half hours, but forty-five minutes is more common today. A light meal and sweets are served, the guests retire to the garden, then, at the sound of a gong, they return for tea. Usually a light or thin tea is also served to end the ceremony. Written invitations are extended and the host is involved in scrupulous preparation. One can hardly imagine a dust mote in the vicinity.

To describe the whole ceremony is not only lengthy but fails to do justice to the economy of movement, ritualistic pace, and minute detail in every act. Words cannot express the near balletlike intensity of the event. Rather, here are examples of how extensively every step is formalized.

THE GUESTS

When the guests arrive, dressed in appropriately subdued colors, they wait in an area across the garden for the host. After they are assembled, the host, who has remained in the teahouse, emerges, approaches them silently, bows, and returns to the teahouse. They follow, single file, led by one of the guests who has been chosen to be the leader. Walking across the path, they bring their attention to the beauty of the garden, which is a spare Zen rendering of the perfect harmony of nature. Symbolically, they are making the transition from worldly concerns to the moment of tea.

At the approach to the teahouse there is a water basin for washing. Each guest steps up in order and washes in accordance with the etiquette of Japanese purification rites: first the left hand, then the right, symbolically cleansing the heart and body, shedding the impurities of the outer world. They enter the teahouse, crouching through a low doorway, a humbling ritual seen as a leveling of rank, making all people equal. They enter in a single file, and when they leave, they depart in reverse order.

During the actual serving of tea, the guests sit attentively on their knees on their tatami mats. The host walks, in measured movements, back and forth to the preparation room, bringing out the utensils in a specific order: the charcoal for the fire, the kettle, the ladle, the tea caddy, and the tea bowl from which they all will drink. All of this is performed with great precision, and the implements are laid out on the mats

in exact relation to one another for the guests to admire. Indeed, at certain points in the ceremony, they are passed from person to person for respectful appreciation—but only at the prescribed moments.

THE TEA

One by one, the host cleans the immaculate utensils with a silk cloth. His gestures are similar to those of a clergyman handling ritual objects in a place of worship. While the guests enjoy the sound of the water boiling and the charcoal crackling, the host prepares the tea, *matcha,* made with powdered *gyokuro* leaves, the finest of Japanese teas. The host places three scoops of tea in the *chawan*, the bowl, and adds boiling water. Then he whisks rhythmically until the tea is smooth and thick.

The ritual of drinking begins. The leading guest moves forward on his knees and picks up the bowl with his right hand, placing it in the palm of his left, still supporting it with the fingers of his right. He sips, praises the flavor, takes two more sips, and then wipes the rim with a *kaishi,* a small paper napkin he brought with him. Each guest repeats this performance.

As an example of how specific every action is, the following are instructions on how to drink *usucha,* a thin tea served at the end of the ceremony.

Place the chawan *between you and the main guest inside the tatami edging.*
Bow and say, "I will join you."
Place the chawan *between you and the next guest.*

Bow and say, "Excuse me for going before you."
Place the chawan *in front of you inside the tatami*
   edging.
Bow and say, "Thank you for the tea," to the host.
Take the chawan *with your right hand.*
Place the chawan *on your left palm.*
Steady the chawan *with your right hand.*
Bow your head slightly to express thanks.
Turn the chawan *clockwise twice in order to avoid its*
   front.
Drink the tea to the last tip.
Wipe the place where you drank from with your right
   thumb and index finger.
Wipe your fingers on your kaishi.
Turn the chawan *back so that the front faces you.*
Place the chawan *in front of you outside the tatami*
   edging.

SPIRITUAL HARMONY

None of these are meant to be hollow gestures. The intent is
that by concentrating on the procedures of the ceremony, the
participants will attain an experience akin to the spirituality
that is inherent in Zen meditation. The ceremony, Okakuro
wrote, is "an improvised drama whose plot is woven about
the tea, the flowers, and the paintings. Not a colour to disturb
the tone of the room, not a sound to mar the rhythm of things,
not a gesture to obtrude on the harmony, not a word to break
the unity of the surroundings."

Taken all together, the simplicity of the surroundings, the
meditative quality of the movements, the uninterrupted tranquillity, the nearly hypnotic formality of the Japanese Tea

Ceremony create a sense of harmony with the universe, a feeling of oneness with a larger consciousness. The Japanese tea ceremony is *self*-conscious—it is an art form whose contemplation becomes a spiritual act.

English Afternoon Tea: The Social Hour

Love and scandal are the best sweeteners of tea.

—HENRY FIELDING (1707–1754)

Moving from the Japanese Tea Ceremony to an English Afternoon Tea may seem like traveling in time from the sublime to the frivolous, but the English took their tea seriously—not ponderously. Afternoon Tea in the eighteenth and nineteenth century in the drawing rooms of the well-to-do was not to be taken lightly. Women were "At Home" to receive guests on certain days, and those who "called" left their engraved cards on the plate provided in the foyer. Tea was a time for exchanging talk and casting glances, for men paid their respects as well. And with good reason. There were no telephones, and face-to-face conversation, a lost art, some might say, was necessary for communication. There was a great deal to communicate: Gossip, of course, was delightful, and scandal, delicious. The social scales tipped over a cup of tea. But there were events to discuss as well, for CNN did not bring news into the drawing room.

IMPLEMENTS

Being presented with the utensils of a historic English Afternoon Tea is like being faced with too many spoons at the dinner table. You immediately feel as if your etiquette education has failed you. Actually, you were just born too late.

The socially conscious British of the eighteenth and nineteenth centuries knew exactly what to do with a mote spoon and a caddy spoon and other instruments of delicate torture. They used them all the time. The Afternoon Tea was defined by implements as much as it was by tea, for the elegant women who presided over these rituals were as devoted to their possessions as they were to the brew.

The tea itself was kept in a *caddy,* an anglicized version of the Malay word *kati,* meaning, *one pound,* referring to the boxes in which tea made its journey to England. Indeed, the caddy was a box, both functional and decorative, like all tea utensils. Wooden, sometimes beautifully inlaid, caddies held two spaces for two types of tea and sometimes a small cut-glass mixing bowl for mixing tea for the brew. Tea was measured out by short-handled silver caddy spoons, which fit neatly inside. Wrought in wonderful designs, these spoons, like most of this tea equipage, are now the sort of prize collectors hope to discover hiding among the rubble in backwater antique shops. The most elaborate caddy, the *teapoy,* stood on its own like a tea sentinel perched atop a pedestal or three-legged table. As always, objects speak of lives and, in the case of caddies, the telling point is that all had locks and keys. Tea thieves? Well, not necessarily, but there were servants in the house. Tea was not only precious, but expensive, and there seemed no reason to make it a temptation, too.

TEA SERVICE

One wonders why anyone would bother to steal tea when there was so much silver around. The gorgeous silver tea service, coveted by English hostesses of every period, is still the epitome of luxury. To match this metallic opulence, the tea service demanded porcelain, or china, as it was called because of its origins. In the eighteenth century, pottery concerns hustled to create their own porcelain and, indeed, discovered processes with which to match the delicacy and beauty of the Chinese. Many of today's most sought-after antique and contemporary porcelain designs were created on the altar of tea, for they were English renditions of the Chinese and Japanese patterns introduced to the West with tea.

TEA BOWLS AND TEA CUPS

It all began with the teacup or, more accurately, the tea bowl. The first cups to arrive in England were Chinese or Japanese handleless bowls, not exactly a comfortable vessel for holding hot tea for any length of time. This was accompanied by a shallow, rimless saucer and, in the beginning, tea was drunk out of both the cup, called a *can,* and the saucer. Much slurping was involved. By the middle of the eighteenth century, upwardly mobile hostesses were rewarded with the single-handled teacup and a saucer with a recessed depression and rim to keep it from sliding about. These were a much better match for their elegant aspirations.

ESSENTIAL UTENSILS

The teakettle and the teapot evolved equally as beautifully to grace the table in the most pleasing fashion possible. These were accompanied by several other necessary items. Tea strainers, still used today, were miniature works of silver artistry that fit over the cup to catch any leaves that might escape from the pot. The aforementioned mote spoon was a pierced spoon designed to skim off any errant material that might have slipped into the cup. And then there was the inelegantly named slop bowl. Not as graceless as it sounds, the slop bowl was used for spent tea leaves. Naturally, there was a pitcher for milk, a bowl for sugar, and sugar tongs. One lump or two?

TEA FARE

And then there was food. Muffins, of course, were served in their very own muffin dish. Not just any old plate, these were silver, with a high-domed lid and a liner that held hot water—these were *hot* muffins. Already dripping with butter, muffins could still be further dressed with cinnamon or sugar from a handy muffineer, which looked a bit like a domed salt shaker. And to put icing on the cake, or really jam on the scone, there was a pretty glass preserves dish with a spoon. When all this was in place, the hostess was ready.

SERVING TEA

Here is an invitation to Afternoon Tea, circa 1860. A stately tea table would be covered with a lovely embroidered or lace

cloth. Teacups, saucers, and spoons would be arranged symmetrically, each sitting atop an organdy napkin with a plate beneath it. The silver tea service, with large tray, teakettle, teapot, sugar, creamer, slop bowl, and strainer would stand as the *pièce de résistance*. The hostess would sit by the table, mixing and infusing the tea. Guests would be asked what they would like in their tea, and the cup would be filled and passed. If there were servants available, they might convey a plain cup on a tray with a small sugar bowl and creamer to each guest.

Serving tea was not a random act nor was the choice of food. Thin, thin little sandwiches, with bread crusts removed, were filled with egg or cucumber, tomato, jam, or paté. There were muffins and breads, and the famous crumpets and scones. That was for the first cup of tea. The second was accompanied by sweets: iced cakes, fruitcakes, sponge cakes, and French pastries. Generally, there was not a third. Afternoon tea was a ritual with a schedule, a delectable hour, but not an afternoon.

Making Tea Personal: Ceremonies of Your Own

Now stir the fire, and close the shutters fast,
Let fall the curtains, wheel the sofa round,
And, while the bubbling and loud hissing urn
Throws up a steamy column and the cups
That cheer but not inebriate, wait on each,
So let us welcome peaceful evening in.

—WILLIAM COWPER (1731–1800)

Chinese, Japanese, or English, all seem a bit lofty as aspirations for your own tea ceremonies, but in essence, they are not. For it's the essence that counts, and each has something to offer that can be adapted to and enhance your lifestyle, which, after all, is the point of tea. Think of the Chinese tea, loosely translated, as a tea of total relaxation, informality, and self-indulgence. Consider the Japanese tea as a model of elegance with an element of formality and sophistication, a way to use tea to rise above your everyday routine. And the English tea, well, what could be a better model for polishing up the silver, filling up the trays, and spoiling your friends? Tea is never boring.

TEA IN THE CHINESE SPIRIT

In the spirit of Chinese tea, create a regular tea for yourself or a few friends that is like sinking into the cushions of a comfortable couch. This is tea in jeans, tea with feet up, tea with spontaneity but some forethought. Choose a place in the house that you like best to be, not the one that is most practical. Sit where you can look at the room from the angle you enjoy most, or where you can look out the window and get a glimpse of the yard that you never have time to appreciate. Use your favorite mug, the one with the handle that holds all your fingers, and choose a tea that has a taste you love, that will be both invigorating and relaxing, the real magic of tea.

Bring awareness to the tea. See if you can let the steam envelop your face and, at the same time, relax the muscles around your eyes and your jaws. Inhale the tea's aroma and take a deep breath, hold it for a moment, and then let it go, whooshing out all thoughts, leaving room in your mind only for the feeling of hot, fragrant tea and a full awareness of this single, pleasant moment. Make this appointment with yourself daily, weekly, or monthly with your friends. Thich Nhat Hanh, the famous Vietnamese Buddhist monk, says that if you fail to bring your awareness to such moments, you miss your "appointment with life." A tea with this much refreshment is too good to miss.

STYLISHLY JAPANESE TEA

To bring a Japanese tea into your life, consider making tea an occasion for two if there is a significant other in your life or for a like-minded friend who recognizes the restorative value of punctuating everyday life with something out of the ordinary, even something extraordinary. Evening is nice for such times. Prepare a very light supper and make tea and dessert the climax. Looking good is part of the ceremony; no end of the day, letting your hair down demeanor is allowed. Make an effort with yourself and your tea table. There should be flowers and definitely candles, and any of the pieces of tableware that especially please you that you don't normally use. To add a note of formality, choose a place in the house where you usually don't sit, where you generally entertain company.

And act like company. Have everything ready, so you can feel like your own guest as much as possible. Breaking out of your regular routine, the more formal clothes and the less familiar setting will help you take note of your surroundings and each other. Talk to one another and pay attention—just as you would with guests. Make tea as if your relationship depended upon it, serving it with the care necessary to get it just right. Choose a tea that is substantial and deeply satisfying, one that will be enlivening, with a touch of mellowness. The quietness of this tea should inspire you to listen to each other. There should be no other sounds except, perhaps, music that you both like. There should be no other thoughts except the pleasure of each other's company and the tea.

CONVIVIAL ENGLISH TEA

In today's context, an English Afternoon Tea is a party. There doesn't have to be a holiday, it doesn't have to be someone's birthday, but a tea that pulls out all the stops like this one could certainly celebrate an occasion. Here's an opportunity to polish up whatever silver has been hiding in those cloth bags and show it off. Take out your grandmother's china, the crystal bowl you got for a wedding present, and the linen and lace you're going to hate to launder later. It's worth it. All the pomp and frills are going to make guests feel festive. Invite as many people as you imagine you can handle so the conversation will buzz. People spark conviviality in each other when the stage is set and the atmosphere is right.

Make tea a centerpiece. Create some ways, perhaps multiple teapots, to prepare different types of tea, so everyone gets involved in the process—and the tasting. Newcomers are going to be surprised and delighted. The more everyone learns about tea, the more they will enjoy it, and the better the afternoon. Include coffee. And why not wine? Liquor was certainly not unheard of in eighteenth-century England. The food should be ample and varied, anything that can be held in the hand and eaten without a fork. Tea and forks don't work together, and unlike the very British afternoon tea, yours may certainly last more than an hour.

TEA, PERSONALLY

Any amount of time you spend with tea can be a personal ceremony. But tea doesn't need the ceremony, you do. Tea offers the possibilities, and because it has so much to offer, you must take it. Tea, brewed in the morning in a pleasing pot and sipped piping hot for just a very few minutes, will gather your strength for the coming day. Make it a ritual, and the repetition, the fact that you can count on tea, will anchor you before the day begins to fly away. Tea as a break from work, in the morning or the afternoon, will keep your energy lifted if it's high or revive your spirits if they flag. Make this smallest of ceremonies away from whatever chore you are doing, but make it every day. And at night, tea will not lull you to sleep or keep you up, it will bring closure to the day, a necessary ceremony to cut loose from nagging feelings, to forget regrets, and to collect thoughts. Tea, after the dishes are done, after the children are asleep, is the signal that one day is done and that you can look forward to another. These are the most personal and, perhaps, the most meaningful tea ceremonies of all.

The Tea Party: Recipes for Accompaniments

Teacups to Mugs: A Personal Afternoon Tea

There are few hours in life more agreeable than the hour dedicated to the ceremony known as afternoon tea.

—HENRY JAMES (1843–1916),
THE PORTRAIT OF A LADY

Tradition and formality, manners and form are not to be scoffed at. They bring civility to life. Afternoon tea, begun centuries ago, was positively laden with social dictates. But no more. There are still distinctions between informal and formal teas and elaborate descriptions of each can be given down to the last doily, but what is most interesting about tea is what you, yourself, enjoy, and what your own style can bring to the pleasure of drinking tea and entertaining with tea. The buttoned-up ladies who bequeathed us tea etiquette might raise an eyebrow at paper napkins and pottery, but it's time to give them a nod of appreciation for the form they bestowed upon us, and move on. So what follows are the nuts and bolts of putting tea and food on the table for anywhere from ten to fifty guests. The only real rule is that improvisation is allowed.

TEA SERVICE

Start by creating your own tea service. You may be fortunate enough to have inherited your grandmother's silver or unlucky enough to have received her favorite teapot in the shape of a cottage, but whatever you choose, you must have a teapot. The traditional tea service is silver, porcelain, or ceramic and consists of a teapot, an additional kettle for hot water, a pitcher of milk, a bowl for sugar, and a small dish for lemon slices. Depending on where you brew the tea, you may need a small bowl to deposit the used leaves or infuser. Cups and saucers, small plates, and teaspoons must also be on hand, and napkins, too.

Those are the necessities. How you interpret them is a function of the occasion, your lifestyle, and taste. For a person who can't leave the house unless her shoes match her purse, a teapot with accessories in all in the same pattern is practically an involuntary choice—but it's not the only choice. If you prefer formality, take out your wedding china, but if you adore pottery and have a collection of mugs, no two alike, why not give people a chance to admire them, too. If you have a grand appliquéd linen tablecloth, use it to dress the table and the occasion. But if paper napkins look better with your dishes and work better with you laundry schedule, use them to punctuate the table with color.

TEA TABLE

Classically, an informal tea takes place in one room, like the living room where the hostess pours, everyone sits, and the food is passed around. A more formal tea, generally for a larger group, expands into more than one room with the dining room table reserved for presenting tea and food, and the living room the place where people mingle. In that case, tea is offered at one end of the table and coffee and, perhaps, punch at the other, with food assembled strategically. A centerpiece of flowers and candles is never considered too much.

Of course, if you live in a one-and-a-half-room apartment with a pocket-sized dining nook, all such advice is about as relevant as instructions for your next black-tie, sit-down dinner for twenty. That is exactly the point. Classical tea may not be your cup of tea, so feel free to have your tea spread on the kitchen counter, or the deck, or a sideboard in the foyer, which sounds better than the hall, and works just the

same. Never decide *not* to serve tea because the place doesn't seem *right*. There are no wrongs. In fact, entertaining with tea is so easy and affordable and such a fine opportunity to be creative in your own surroundings that it may be very right for you, indeed.

TEA TREATS

Before you focus your creativity on the food, consider what is traditionally served because, in this regard, the form incorporates some lovely common sense. Afternoon tea is generally called for between three and six o'clock; the later the hour, the more substantial the fare. (As a matter of fact, if you invite people with the intention of having them from three to five, make that clear in your invitation. It's a paradox of social intercourse that everyone is most at ease when the parameters are clear.) Classically, three types of food are served, either successively or simultaneously. The initial temptation is comfort food, warm muffins, scones, biscuits, and toasts accompanied by butter and jams. The second is the infamous tea sandwich, the lightest of all possible morsels that can be created from two slices of bread and a dollop of filling. And the last may be first in most people's minds, the sweets of cookies, cakes, and candies. Most must be finger food unless there are few enough people to sit down and use a fork. Having tea shouldn't be a balancing act.

It should be a pleasure, just as it has been for centuries. Adapting afternoon tea to your own style is honoring that tradition. Think of tea being taken all over the world with the imprint of individuality, but affording the same soothing, relaxing, invigorating effect. It may only be an hour in the day, but its influence is so civilizing, so restorative, that it enhances the lives of people everywhere. Even the straitlaced ladies who began it all would approve.

Cucumber Sandwiches to Scones: Tea Delicacies

There are few more agreeable moments in life than tea in an English country house in winter. It is dark at four o'clock. The Family and guests come in from the cold air. The curtains are drawn, the open wood fire is blazing, the people sit down around the table and with a delightful meal—for the most attractive food in England is served at afternoon tea—drink of the cheering beverage.

—WILLIAM LYON PHELPS, 1930

SCONES

Scones are the quintessential English afternoon tea accompaniment. The British have a way of eating them with just the right dabs and swirls of butter, jam, and, in some parts of the country, clotted cream. Knead them for less than a minute and they will achieve their single texture—both light and substantial, a mouthful that neither melts nor crunches but satisfies—the reason the Dutch named them *schoonbrot,* or *beautiful bread,* from which the name scone is derived. Crumpets are another matter, English muffin–like creations that can be eaten hot right out of the oven or kept till the next day and toasted with jam or honey. Crumpets may be less famous for their taste than ''tea and crumpets,'' which is synonymous with afternoon tea.

SCONES

    2 cups flour
    1 tablespoon baking powder
    ½ teaspoon salt
    2 tablespoons confectioners' sugar
    1 egg
    ⅓ cup milk
    5 tablespoons unsalted butter

Preheat oven to 450° F. Place an ungreased baking sheet in the oven. Sift together the flour, baking powder, salt, and confectioners' sugar. In a small bowl, add the egg to the milk and blend well. Cut the butter into the dry ingredients until the mixture resembles coarse cornmeal. Make a well in the center, and stir in the milk and egg mixture. Blend lightly with a fork until just moistened and a soft dough is formed. Turn onto a floured surface. Knead very briefly and very lightly to form a loose, smooth dough. Roll out or pat out to a thickness of ½" to ¾". Cut into small triangles or cut with a 2" cookie cutter. Use a spatula to transfer to hot cookie sheet. Bake 8 to 10 minutes or until golden brown. Makes about 12 scones.

Note: For variety, try fruit scones or for a savory version, try cheese scones. For fruit scones, add to the flour ¼ teaspoonfuls of whatever spices you like (cinnamon, nutmeg, or cloves, for example) and 1 cup of raisins or other dried fruit like currants. For cheese scones, add 1 cup of Cheddar cheese plus ½ teaspoon of dried mustard.

BATCH SCONES

    2 cups flour
    1 tablespoon baking powder
    8 ounces unsalted butter

¼ cup cold vegetable shortening
¾ cup confectioners' sugar
½ cup raisins
½ cup dates, pitted and chopped
1 egg
¼ cup milk
   Granulated sugar

Preheat oven to 375° F. Place an ungreased baking sheet in the oven. Sift together flour and baking powder. With your fingers, combine with butter and shortening until the mixture is crumbly. Stir in sugar, raisins, and dates. Beat the egg and milk together. Stir gently into the dry ingredients with a fork until a soft dough forms. Turn onto a floured surface and knead very briefly and very lightly. Shape into a ball. Place on the hot baking sheet and flatten to about 1" thick. Score into 8–12 wedges with a sharp knife. Sprinkle with sugar. Bake about 25 minutes or until golden brown. Let cool 5 minutes and cut into wedges. Serve with butter. Best when eaten warm.

CRUMPETS

Crumpets are, by definition, round, and they are made with crumpet rings on a griddle. To improvise, use 3" cookie cutters and a heavy frying pan.

1½ cups warm water
 2 cups flour
 1 package yeast
 1 teaspoon confectioners' sugar
½ teaspoon baking soda
 1 teaspoon salt
¾ cup milk

Pour the water into a 2-quart bowl. Sift half the flour and add it with the yeast and sugar to the bowl. Allow to stand until frothy, about 20 minutes. Add the baking soda, salt, the rest of the flour, and ½ cup of the milk. Beat well. Add more milk, if necessary, to make the batter thick, but able to be poured. Grease the griddle and the rings. Heat however many rings will fit on the griddle until hot. Pour about 2 tablespoons of batter into each ring. Cook until holes appear, about 10 minutes. Remove the rings, turn over the crumpets, and cook again about 10 minutes. Makes about 16 crumpets.

TEA SANDWICHES

The afternoon tea sandwich is not a meal. It is more like a savory confection, a tease of a taste, a tidbit, a morsel. It is not meant to be satisfying as much as it is satisfactory, and some can be very satisfactory, indeed. Tea sandwiches are, by definition, small and delicate. The bread is always thin and the filling sparing, but this doesn't preclude them from being delicious. Anyone who mocks a cucumber sandwich as a food equivalent to a crust of bread has never had a real tea sandwich. Tea sandwiches *never* have crusts.

Constructing tea sandwiches does involve cutting off crusts and a few steps that are a bit more elaborate than slapping ham and cheese between two pieces of bread. To begin, buy an unsliced, firm-textured white bread. The first step is *slicing*, which is often easier if the bread has been in the freezer for an hour or two. The second step is *buttering*, which is accomplished as you slice. Tea sandwiches have some type of spread, usually butter-based, on each slice, in addition to the filling. It is much easier if the spread is prepared in advance and ready at room temperature. Take the bread from the freezer and slice off one end with a long, serrated or electric, knife. Cover the cut face of the loaf with the butter spread. Use a small-bladed, flexible knife. Make a thin slice, spread again, and cut. In this way, each slice will be covered with spread as you slice.

To make the sandwiches, take two slices, buttered side up. Spread a thin layer of filling on one slice. Cover with the second slice, buttered side down. For an elegant presentation, the crusts must be removed. Then cut each sandwich into four squares or triangles or three finger-sized pieces. Ultimate tea sandwiches can be cut with cookie cutters in shapes to suit your fancy, such as hearts, diamonds, ovals, and rounds.

Fancier still are pinwheel sandwiches. For these, begin by cutting off the crust of the whole bread. Then spread butter along the *length* of one side. Make as thin a slice as possible on this long side and use the same system, spreading as you slice. In addition, lay the slices on a damp kitchen towel as you work to keep them from drying out and turning up at the edges. Spread a thin layer of filling on each slice and then roll them up lengthwise, jelly roll style. Wrap each roll separately to freeze or place in the refrigerator. Cut them chilled (or straight from the freezer, if frozen) close to serving time by cutting crosswise in thin slices.

Each of the following recipes includes a spread that complements the fillings. These, being a matter of taste, are optional and interchangeable. Plain butter, softened, can be used, and any flavored butter that appeals to you is fine.

CUCUMBER SANDWICHES

Cucumbers

    1–2 cucumbers (about 12" of cucumber)
        Salt
     1 tablespoon olive oil
     2 teaspoons lemon juice
     1 teaspoon confectioners' sugar
    ¼ teaspoon white pepper

Creamed Butter

   12 tablespoons unsalted butter, room temperature

   1 tablespoon heavy cream
   ¼ teaspoon Dijon mustard
   1 tablespoon lemon juice

Blend all ingredients until soft and spreadable.

Note: This spread recipe can be proportionately increased for larger amounts.

Cut off ends of cucumber and score the sides with the tines of a fork. Slice as thin as possible, preferably with a food processor. Lightly salt the slices and place them in a colander, weigh them down with a bowl or plate, and let them drain for an hour or two. Pat dry. If time is short, place them on a paper towel to drain. In a bowl, combine cucumber slices, oil, lemon juice, sugar, and pepper. Spread thin slices of bread with creamed butter. Cover half the slices of bread with cucumber slices. Top with other half of bread. Slice into triangles.

SHRIMP SANDWICHES

   20 slices bread
    8 ounces cream cheese, beaten
    1 cup finely chopped, cooked shrimp
   ¼ cup scallions, finely chopped
       Salt and fresh pepper to taste

Parsley Butter
   16 ounces (2 sticks) unsalted butter, room temperature
    1 teaspoon salt
   ¼ teaspoon white pepper
   ¼ cup very finely chopped parsley

Combine all filling ingredients until they form a spreadable consistency. Spread half the slices of bread with parsley butter and then shrimp filling. Cover with second slice of bread. Slice in whatever shape desired.

CREAM CHEESE, CELERY, AND CHIVE SANDWICHES

20 slices bread
 8 ounces cream cheese, beaten
 ½ cup celery, finely minced
 ¼ cup chives, finely chopped
   Salt and freshly ground pepper to taste

Horseradish Butter
16 ounces (2 sticks) unsalted butter, room temperature
 1 tablespoon white horseradish, drained well
 1 teaspoon lemon juice
 1 teaspoon sugar

Combine all filling ingredients until they form a spreadable consistency. Spread half the slices of bread with horseradish butter and then filling. Cover with second slice of bread. Slice in whatever shape desired.

EGG AND WATERCRESS SANDWICHES

20 slices bread
 ½ cup watercress, finely chopped
 5 hard-boiled eggs
 1 teaspoon Dijon mustard
   Heavy cream to bind
   Salt and pepper to taste

Garlic Butter
 2 cloves garlic, blanched and put through a press

16 ounces unsalted butter, room temperature
1 teaspoon lemon juice
    Salt and pepper to taste

Be sure the watercress is washed and thoroughly dried
before chopping. Combine all filling ingredients until
they form a spreadable consistency. Spread half the slices
of bread with garlic butter and then filling. Cover with
second slice of bread. Slice in whatever shape desired.

TEA BREADS

The tea bread speaks for itself as an afternoon tea food. Less
sweet than cake, but more dessertlike than bread, tea breads
are the perfect in-between pleasure. Especially easy to make,
they freeze and keep well and stand ever ready for an im-
promptu tea. Date and nut bread can do double duty as a
sandwich bread with a cream cheese filling. The lemon has
just a pucker of tartness and the banana is far more than a
repository for overripe fruit. It's so good there's never any
left to keep.

DATE AND NUT BREAD

2½ cups flour
1 cup sugar
3 teaspoons baking powder

    1 teaspoon salt
    1 egg
    3 tablespoons vegetable oil
    1 teaspoon vanilla
 1¼ cups milk
    1 cup dates, pitted and chopped
 ¾ cup walnuts, chopped

Preheat oven to 350° F. Grease a 9" × 5" × 3" loaf pan. Mix flour, sugar, baking powder, and salt in one bowl, combining with a fork. Mix egg, oil, vanilla, and milk in a larger bowl. Blend the dry ingredients into the egg mixture, scraping the sides and bottom of the bowl. Beat just until blended and do not overbeat. Add dates and nuts and stir in thoroughly. Turn into greased loaf pan. Bake about 1 hour or until tester, inserted in center, comes out clean. Cool in pan 10 minutes. Remove.

LEMON TEA BREAD

    2 cups flour
    2 teaspoons baking powder
 ¼ teaspoon salt
 ¾ cup sugar
 ½ cup milk
    4 tablespoons unsalted butter, room temperature
    1 egg
    2 tablespoons grated lemon rind

Preheat oven to 375° F. Grease a 9" × 5" × 3" loaf pan. With a fork, stir together the flour, baking powder, and salt in a bowl. In a larger bowl, mix the sugar, milk, butter, and egg together until well blended. Gradually stir the milk and egg mixture into the dry ingredients until smooth. Stir in lemon rind. Turn the batter into the pan. Bake about 50 minutes or until the edges turn brown and the cake is golden.

BANANA BREAD

1½ cups flour
¾ cup sugar
½ teaspoon salt
1 teaspoon baking soda
8 ounces unsalted butter
2 eggs
2 teaspoons lemon juice
¼ cup milk
1 cup ripe, mashed banana (2–3 bananas)
½ cup pecans or walnuts, chopped

Preheat oven to 375° F. Grease a 9" × 5" × 3" loaf pan. Combine flour, sugar, salt, and baking soda in a small bowl. Stir with a fork until blended. In a large bowl, beat butter until fluffy. Blend in eggs, lemon juice, milk, and bananas, beating very briefly. Mixing with a fork or wooden spoon, blend the dry ingredients into the egg and banana mixture. Fold in nuts. Turn into pan. Bake 55–60 minutes or until bread springs back when touched lightly in the center. Cool before removing from pan.

COOKIES

Here are light, crisp cookies, rich, moist bars, and dense, creamy tarts. Samples of the variety of afternoon tea, they are meant to be inspiration as much as choices. They are the range within which you can extrapolate, creating your own assortment. Among these, the delicious Scottish shortbread is traditional, a plain cookie with enough character to stand up to any confection. The cracker cookies are those least likely to be found on an English table, but they are irresistible, nearly addictive, and an appreciated addition at any time.

ALMOND COOKIES

Here is something to offer your most virtuous friends: a cookie low in cholesterol, fat, and calories, and still delicious.

2½ cups flour
1 teaspoon baking powder
¼ teaspoon salt
1 egg
¾ cup sugar
1 cup vegetable oil
2–3 teaspoons almond extract
1 teaspoon vanilla

Topping

Blanched (or unblanched) whole almonds, 1 for each cookie
1 egg plus 1 tablespoon water, lightly beaten together

Preheat oven to 350° F. Lightly grease cookie sheets. Sift together flour, baking powder, and salt. In a large bowl, beat egg well. Add sugar and blend well. Add oil, almond extract, and vanilla, beating briefly. Gradually add dry ingredients, beating lightly. If the batter becomes too thick, combine by hand with a rubber spatula. Form into ¾" balls. Place on slightly greased cookie sheet, 2" apart. They will expand. Press almond into center of each cookie. Brush on egg topping. Bake until delicately browned, 15–20 minutes. The time will depend on how big the cookies are. Makes about 3 dozen.

CRESCENT COOKIES

    8 ounces unsalted butter
    ¼ cup confectioners' sugar
    2 teaspoons vanilla
    1 teaspoon water
    2 cups flour, sifted
    1 cup pecans, chopped

Preheat oven to 300° F. Cream the butter and sugar. Add
vanilla and water and blend briefly. Gradually add flour,
blending a little at a time. Stir in the nuts. Chill for 30
minutes. Roll between hands to form small cylinders
about 1½" long. Shape into crescents. Place on ungreased cookie sheet. Bake 20 minutes or until delicately
browned. Makes about 3 dozen.

SCOTTISH SHORTBREAD

    2 cups flour
    ¼ cup cornstarch
    ¼ teaspoon salt
    8 ounces unsalted butter, room temperature
    1 cup confectioners' sugar
    2 tablespoons granulated sugar

Preheat oven to 325° F. Sift flour, cornstarch, and salt
together in one bowl. In a large bowl, cream butter and
confectioners' sugar until light and fluffy. Gradually fold
dry ingredients into butter mixture. Press dough into an
ungreased baking dish, 11" × 7" or 9" × 9". Prick the
entire surface with a fork. With a sharp knife, lightly score
the dough into about 20 pieces. Bake about 30 minutes
or until lightly browned around the edges and pale

golden. Sprinkle with sugar. Cool 10 minutes in pan and cut into pieces.

GINGERSNAPS

2¼ cups flour
1 tablespoon ground ginger
2 teaspoons baking soda
1 teaspoon cinnamon
½ teaspoon salt
6 tablespoons unsalted butter
1 cup brown sugar
1 egg
¼ cup molasses
Granulated sugar

Preheat oven to 375° F. Lightly grease baking sheet. Sift flour, ginger, baking soda, cinnamon, and salt into one bowl. Cream butter until soft, then add brown sugar gradually, blending until fluffy. Beat in egg and molasses. Add dry ingredients a little at a time until well blended. Shape dough by scant teaspoonfuls into balls. Dip tops into granulated sugar. Place sugared side up, 2" apart, on lightly greased cookie sheet. Bake 10–15 minutes or until set. Cool on baking sheet. Makes about 4 dozen.

ORANGE COOKIES

8 ounces unsalted butter, room temperature
½ teaspoon salt
1 cup sugar
1 egg
1 tablespoon orange juice

    Grated rind of 1 orange
1½ cups flour

Preheat oven to 375° F. Cream butter with salt until fluffy, and gradually add sugar until well blended. Add egg and blend well. Add orange juice and rind and blend. Add flour a little at a time. Do not overbeat. Drop rounded teaspoonfuls of dough onto ungreased cookie sheet about 2" apart. Bake 10 minutes or until edges are golden. Cool on cookie sheet briefly. Makes about 4 dozen.

CRACKER COOKIES

    Unsalted saltine crackers
8 ounces unsalted butter
½ cup sugar
1 12-ounce package chocolate chips
1 cup of chopped walnuts or pecans

Preheat oven to 350° F. Line a cookie sheet with sides with foil. Place crackers on the sheet so that they line the entire bottom. Break off some to fill spaces if necessary. In a small saucepan, melt butter over low heat. Stir in sugar. Remove from heat. Pour butter/sugar mixture over crackers as evenly as possible. Bake 10 minutes. Remove from the oven and sprinkle chocolate chips (as evenly as possible) over the crackers. Turn off the oven. Return the cookie sheet to the oven for just 2 minutes to melt the chocolate. Remove. Spread the chocolate evenly over the crackers with a flexible spreader. Sprinkle chopped nuts on top of chocolate. Refrigerate overnight or several hours. Break into pieces with a knife. The shapes will be very irregular, looking more like broken pieces of candy than cookies.

MINIATURE PECAN TARTS

Tart Cups

1 3-ounce package cream cheese, room temperature
8 tablespoons unsalted butter, room temperature
1 cup flour, sifted

Filling

1 egg
¾ cup brown sugar
1 tablespoon butter, softened
1 teaspoon vanilla
¼ teaspoon salt
⅔ cup chopped pecans

Preheat oven to 325° F. Blend cream cheese and butter. Lightly blend in flour. Chill for at least 1 hour. Shape into 2 dozen 1" balls. Place in tiny, 1¾", ungreased muffin tins. Press dough onto bottom and sides of cups. Beat together the egg, sugar, butter, vanilla, and salt until smooth. Place half the pecans in the pastry-lined cups. Fill the cups with the egg mixture, and top with the remaining pecans. Do not overfill; filling that runs over will cause the tarts to stick to the pan. Bake for 25 minutes or until set. Remove from pan by running knife along edge and prodding loose with a tablespoon. Makes 24 tarts.

TINY CHEESECAKE TARTS

Tart Crust

¾ cup graham cracker crumbs
2 tablespoons sugar
2 tablespoons butter, melted

Filling

           8 ounces cream cheese
          ¼ cup sugar
          ¼ teaspoon cornstarch
          ½ teaspoon vanilla
           1 egg
              Canned fruit pie filling

Preheat oven to 350° F. *To make crust:* In a small bowl, mix graham cracker crumbs, sugar, and butter. Place midget cupcake papers in 1¾" muffin tins. Press 1 tablespoon crumb mixture into each paper. *To make filling:* Combine cream cheese, sugar, cornstarch, vanilla, and egg, and beat until creamy. Place 1 tablespoon of this mixture over the crumbs in each paper cup. Bake 10 minutes or until firm. When done, top with cherry or other fruit pie filling from which most of the juice has been drained. Makes 24 tarts.

RASPBERRY BARS

There are two steps to build these delightful bars. The top layer is a simple meringue, which is merely beaten egg whites and sugar. But the eggs must be at room temperature or they will refuse to rise to the occasion.

Crust

           1 cup flour
          ½ teaspoon salt
          ¼ teaspoon baking soda
           8 ounces unsalted butter, room temperature
          ½ cup sugar
              Grated rind of 1 lemon
           2 egg yolks

Topping

    1 cup raspberry jam
    2 egg whites
    ¼ cup sugar
    ½ cup chopped nuts

Preheat oven to 350° F. Grease a 12" × 8" × 2" baking pan. Sift together flour, salt, and baking soda. Blend butter, sugar, and lemon rind. Lightly beat the egg yolks. Add to butter and sugar, and blend. Spread evenly in the greased baking pan. Spread raspberry jam over the batter. Beat the egg whites until foamy. Continue beating, gradually adding the sugar, one tablespoon at a time. Beat until stiff. Fold in the nuts. Spread the meringue over the jam. Bake 35–45 minutes. Cool 5 minutes. Loosen at the edges. Cool a little longer. Cut into strips or squares.

COCONUT BARS

Crust

    8 ounces unsalted butter, room temperature
    ½ cup light brown sugar
    1 cup flour, sifted

Topping

    2 eggs
    1 teaspoon vanilla
    1 cup light brown sugar
    ¼ cup flour
  3½ ounces shredded coconut
    1 cup chopped pecans

Preheat oven to 375° F. Grease a 13" × 9" × 2" baking pan. Combine butter and sugar, and blend well. Add flour and mix well. Pat into greased pan. Bake 12 minutes. Meanwhile, prepare topping. Lightly beat the eggs. Add the vanilla and blend. Briefly blend in the sugar. Stir in the coconut and pecans. Spread over baked crust. Bake 20 minutes longer. Cool 5 minutes. Loosen the edges. Cool. Cut into bars.

LEMON SQUARES

Crust
    8 ounces unsalted butter
    ¼ cup confectioners' sugar
    1 cup flour
    ¼ teaspoon salt

Filling
    2 eggs
    1 cup sugar
    ½ teaspoon baking powder
    2 tablespoons flour
    3 tablespoons fresh lemon juice
    2 teaspoons grated lemon rind
      Confectioners' sugar

Preheat oven to 350° F. *To make crust:* Cream butter and sugar until well blended. Add flour and salt and blend. Pat into bottom of ungreased 8" × 8" × 2" pan. Bake 20 minutes, until lightly browned. *Filling:* Beat together eggs, sugar, baking powder, flour, lemon juice, and rind until fluffy. Pour over hot crust. Bake until set, about 20–25 minutes. Sprinkle with confectioners' sugar.

CAKES

Everyone has their own sweet tooth barometer, and one of the joys of tea is sharing your favorite indulgences with your friends. Here are two cakes, disguised with the plain-Jane, upright names of *coffee* and *pound* that are so much more than the traditional that they border on the decadent. Both go perfectly with tea, and their richness is a luxurious surprise. Since forks are not strictly part of serving tea, it is possible to cut these cakes into finger-sized pieces, but it may be worth breaking the rules to offer a truly gratifying slice of these delicious cakes.

COFFEE CAKE

Cake Batter

      2 cups flour
      1 tablespoon baking powder
     ¼ teaspoon salt
     12 tablespoons of butter (1½ sticks)
    1¼ cups granulated sugar
      2 eggs beaten
    1½ cups sour cream
      1 tablespoon vanilla extract

Nut Mixture

     ¼ cup granulated sugar
     ¼ cup brown sugar
      2 cups pecans, chopped
      1 tablespoon cinnamon

Preheat oven to 350° F. Grease and lightly flour a 10" Bundt pan or springform pan. Sift flour, baking powder, and salt together. Set aside. *For Nut Mixture:* Combine the granulated and brown sugars with pecans and cinnamon. Set aside. Cream butter and sugar well. Add eggs, mix well. Add sour cream and vanilla, mix well. Fold in dry ingredients and beat until just blended. Place half the batter in the pan. Sprinkle with half the nut mixture. Add the remaining batter and cover with rest of nut mixture. Bake about 60 minutes or until a tester inserted in the center comes out clean.

POUND CAKE

  3 tablespoons milk
  3 large eggs
  1 teaspoon vanilla extract
1½ cups flour, sifted
 ½ cup sugar
 ¾ teaspoon baking powder
 ¼ teaspoon salt
 12 tablespoons unsalted butter, room temperature

Preheat oven to 350° F. Grease a 9" × 5" loaf pan (6-cup). Line the bottom with waxed paper and grease and lightly flour the paper. In one bowl, combine the milk, eggs, and vanilla. In a larger bowl, combine the flour, sugar, baking powder, and salt. Blend briefly. Add the butter and ½ the milk mixture. Blend well on low speed. Gradually add the rest of the milk mixture, being sure to scrape the sides and combine all the ingredients. Pour into the pan, smoothing the top. Bake about 60 minutes or until a tester inserted in the center comes out clean. Check earlier for doneness.

Hot Toddy to Iced Mint: A Tea Medley

Its liquor is like the sweetest dew from Heaven.

—LU YÜ (EIGHTH CENTURY),
THE CLASSIC OF TEA

To inveterate tea drinkers, tea is the total beverage. Devotees are willing to take their tea hot, cold, spiked—and adulterated. Tea is so versatile and adaptable that it easily combines with other flavors. When tea is mixed with spices or fruit juices or liquor, a metamorphosis takes place. The tea is changed, yet somehow maintains its character, and the other ingredients are mellowed without losing their own qualities. Finally, as often happens with melding, the whole is quite appealingly different than the sum of the parts.

What follows are a few samples of tea in tandem with other tastes. The hot drinks are made for legendary moments by the fire that call for warmth from the inside out and a touch of sweet and spice to match the mood. The iced teas bring to mind the mythical veranda on which no one lounges anymore. But if a cool sip of these refreshing drinks transports you to a place of languid relaxation, they are definitely worth making. In fact, you can put together tea and almost anything else that beckons to your taste buds and your imagination.

SUGAR SYRUP

Especially with iced tea, dissolving the sugar evenly can be difficult. To solve the problem, here is a sugar syrup that can be can kept on hand indefinitely, ever ready to sweeten beautifully. The lemon syrup is particularly pleasant with both hot and iced teas.

2¼ cups confectioners' sugar
  2 cups cold water

In a saucepan, combine sugar and water, and bring to a boil over medium heat. Simmer for about 10 minutes or until clear. Keep in a tightly sealed container in the refrigerator. Can be stored without time limit.

LEMON SYRUP

    Juice of 3 lemons
  3 cups confectioners' sugar
    Grated rind of 1 lemon
  ½ cup boiling water

Combine all ingredients except boiling water in saucepan and bring to a boil, stirring constantly. Strain and add boiling water. Stir well. Keep in a tightly sealed container in the refrigerator. Use 1 teaspoon or more for desired flavor in iced or hot tea.

HOT HARVEST TEA

  4 cups of hot black tea
  ¼ cup confectioners' sugar or sugar syrup to taste
  1 cup fresh orange juice
  2 cups apple cider
    Grated rind of one lemon

Brew tea. In a large saucepan, pour hot tea over sugar or

sugar syrup. Stir to dissolve. Add orange juice, apple cider, and lemon rind. Heat through. Test for sweetness and add more sugar if desired. Heat to dissolve. Serve hot. Makes 4–6 servings.

HOT MULLED TEA TODDY

    8 cups of cold water
    4 cloves
    1 cinnamon stick
    8 tablespoons of black tea like Darjeeling or Ceylon
 1½ cups pineapple juice
   ½ cup fresh lemon juice
       Grated rind of 1 orange
    1 cup of rum or to taste (optional)
       Honey to taste

Combine water, cloves, and cinnamon stick in a large saucepan. Gradually bring to a boil and simmer briefly. Place tea leaves in a large bowl. Pour water over leaves and brew for 5–7 minutes. Strain back into saucepan. Add pineapple and lemon juices and orange rind. Add rum, if desired. Reheat, but do not boil. Stir in honey to taste. Serve hot. Makes 8 to 10 servings.

CHAI BLEND

    4 cups water
    4 tablespoons black tea
    8 cloves
   ¼ teaspoon ground cardamom
   ½ teaspoon ground ginger
    8 ounces half-and-half or milk

Honey or sugar to taste

Boil water. Brew tea 5–7 minutes. Strain into saucepan. Add cloves, cardamom, and ginger and simmer for 10 minutes. Add half-and-half or milk and heat through, but do not boil. Sweeten to taste with honey or sugar.

ICED MINT TEA

        2 cups cold water
        ½ cup confectioners' sugar
    ¼–½ cup fresh mint leaves, lightly packed
        8 cups water
        8 tablespoons black tea like English Breakfast
            Mint sprigs for garnish

Boil 8 cups of water. Brew tea 5–7 minutes. Strain into pitcher. Combine 2 cups of water, confectioners' sugar, and mint leaves in a small saucepan over medium heat. Stir until sugar dissolves, bring to a boil, and boil about 5 minutes or until just syrupy. Cool. Strain into pitcher with tea and stir. Serve over ice garnished with sprigs of mint. Makes 6–8 servings.

ICED CRANBERRY TEA

        4 cups of cold water
        ¼ teaspoon cinnamon
        ¼ teaspoon nutmeg
        4 tablespoons of black tea like Darjeeling or Ceylon
        ½ cup confectioners' sugar or sugar syrup to taste
        4 cups cranberry juice
        ½ cup orange juice
        ½ cup lemon juice

Lemon slices for garnish

Boil water. Pour over tea and spices in a large bowl or pitcher. Brew 5–7 minutes. Stir in sugar. Add cranberry, orange, and lemon juice. Taste for sweetness. Chill. Serve over ice garnished with lemon slices. Makes 6–8 servings.

ICED LIME TEA

- 8 cups of water
- 8 tablespoons of black tea like Darjeeling or Ceylon
  Juice of 2 limes
- 4 tablespoons of maraschino cherry juice
- ½ cup confectioners' sugar or sugar syrup to taste
  Twists of lime and cherries for garnish

Brew tea and cool. Pour into pitcher. Add lime and cherry juices. Add sugar and stir well. Taste for sweetness. Serve with a twist of lime and a cherry. Makes 6–8 servings.

ICED GREEN TEA SPARKLERS

GREEN TEA APPLE SPARKLER

- 2 cups of cold water
- 2 tablespoons of green tea
- 2 cups apple juice
- 2 cups sparkling water

Boil water. Brew tea for 5–7 minutes. Strain into pitcher. Add apple juice and sparkling water. If sweetness is desired, add sugar syrup, lemon syrup, or confectioners' sugar to taste. Pour over ice to serve. Makes 4–6 servings.

GREEN TEA GINGER SPARKLER

    2 cups of cold water
    2 tablespoons of green tea
    2 tablespoons crystallized ginger, finely chopped
    4 cups ginger ale

Boil water. Brew tea for 5–7 minutes. Strain into covered container. Add ginger, and refrigerate several hours. Strain into pitcher. Add ginger ale. Pour over ice to serve. Makes 4–6 servings.

Bibliography

Blofeld, John, *The Chinese Art of Tea*, Shambala Publications, Inc., Boston, 1985.

Bown, Deni, *Encyclopedia of Herbs & Their Uses*, Dorling Kindersley, London, 1995.

Campbell, Dawn L., *The Tea Book*, Pelican Publishing Company, Gretna, La., 1995.

Clark, Garth, *The Eccentric Teapot*, Abbeville Publishers, New York, 1989.

Garland, Sarah, *The Complete Book of Herbs & Spices*, The Viking Press, New York, 1979.

Gordon, Lesley, *A Country Herbal*, Mayflower Books, New York, 1980.

Huxley, Gervas, *Talking of Tea*, John Wagner & Sons, Ivyland, Pa., 1956.

Hynes, Angela, *The Pleasures of Afternoon Tea*, HPBooks, Inc., New York, 1987.

Kakuzo, Okakura, *The Book of Tea*, Charles E. Tuttle Company, Vermont, 1906, 1956.

Kaufman, William I., *The Tea Cookbook*, Doubleday & Company, New York, 1966.

Lu Yü, *The Classic of Tea*, translated by Francis Ross Carpenter, Little, Brown and Company, Boston, 1974.

Maitland, Derek, *5,000 Years of Tea, A Pictorial Companion*,

W. H. Smith Publishers, Inc., New York, 1982.

Pratt, James Norwood, *The Tea Lover's Companion*, Carol Publishing Group, New York, 1996.

Schafer, Charles and Violet, *Teacraft: A Treasury of Romance, Rituals & Recipes*, Yerba Buena Press, San Francisco, 1975

Schapira, Joel, David, and Karl, *The Book of Coffee & Tea*, St. Martin's Press, New York, 1975, 1982.

Shalleck, Jamie, *Tea*, The Viking Press, New York, 1972.

Smith, Michael, *The Afternoon Tea Book*, Atheneum, New York, 1986.

Ukers, William H., *The Romance of Tea*, Alfred Knopf, New York, 1936.

Woodward, Nancy Hyden, *Teas of the World*, Collier Macmillan Publishers, New York, 1980.